Crescent Color Guide to
Photography

Crescent Color Guide to
Photography

Don Morley

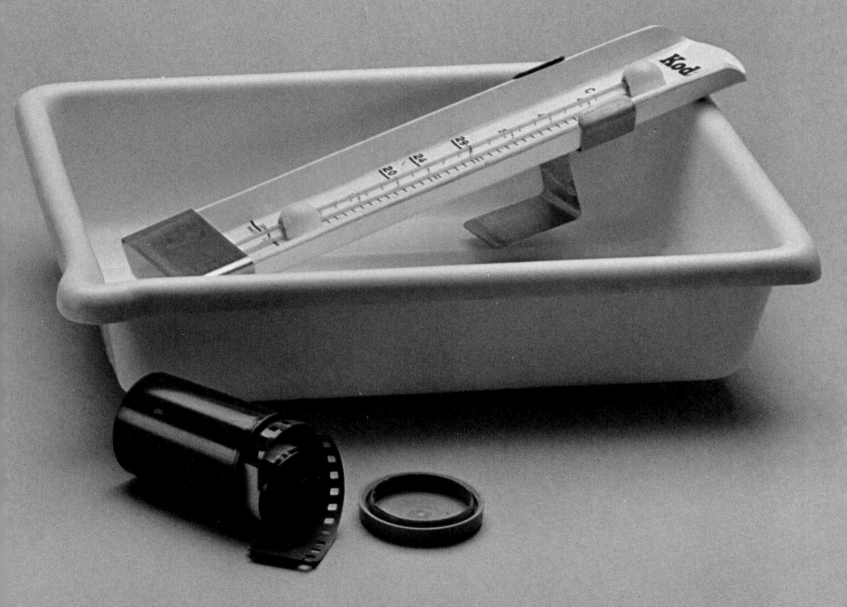

Crescent Books
New York

Photographic acknowledgments
(All-Sport, Morden: 46. Tony Duffy, Morden: 20
bottom, 36, 50 top left. Hamlyn Group Picture Library:
13. Eamon McCabe, London: 31. Robert McMahon,
Surbiton: 43 left. Adrian Murrell, Morden: 34 top.
Steve Perkins, Droitwich: 16 top. Michael Plomer: front
cover, endpapers and title spread. Steve Powell,
Morden: 41 bottom. Tony Taylor, Headley Down: 23,
39 top, 47 top)

All other photographs by Don Morley

Illustrations are by John Green/Groom & Pickerill.

Copyright © The Hamlyn Publishing Group Limited 1982

First English edition published by
The Hamlyn Publishing Group Limited
London · New York · Sydney · Toronto
Astronaut House, Feltham, Middlesex, England

Library of Congress Catalog Card Number: 82-71420

This edition is published by Crescent Books
Distributed by Crown Publishers, Inc.
h g f e d c b a

Printed in Italy

Contents

First Steps in Photography

Most people buy their first camera to record highlights from their own lives. Children and parents, hobbies and holidays provide the initial motivation to take photographs rather than an interest in photography itself. Sadly, those early photographic results are often very disappointing and, perhaps only for want of a little advice and encouragement, many beginners never try again.

The aim of this book is not to persuade the beginner to become a budding professional overnight, or to boost sales of unwanted photographic equipment; rather it aims to show just how simple it is to reverse those inevitable early disappointments. However, one word of caution, especially to the beginner: study and purchase wisely. Even the more advanced enthusiast would be well advised never to buy additional photographic equipment until he or she knows precisely what is needed. Remember: if you don't really understand it, you most certainly don't need it.

Buying photographic equipment today can be like entering a minefield; a thousand and one dealers and manufacturers try to trap you with a never-ending stream of cameras and accessories, all of which in their considered opinion you, the buyer, cannot possibly afford to be without.

To those who have yet to buy that first dream camera or extra lens, the best advice is to 'make haste slowly', and stick to the internationally known manufacturers, for even their cheaper products are made to those companies'

A bathtime photograph of the author's son taken by available light from an adjacent window and using a simple camera with standard lens. This type of scene, with its mixture of light and shade, is an ideal subject for automatic exposure.

For this photograph flash has been used, not from the camera position, but held high above so as not to cast a shadow.

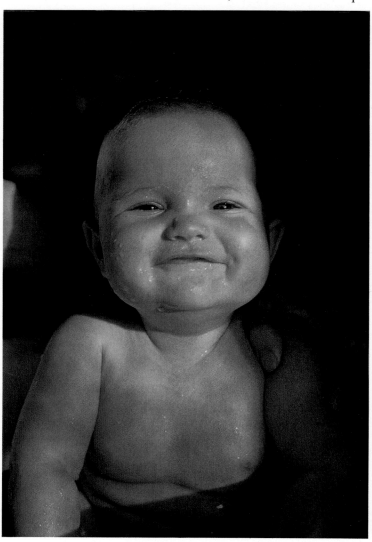

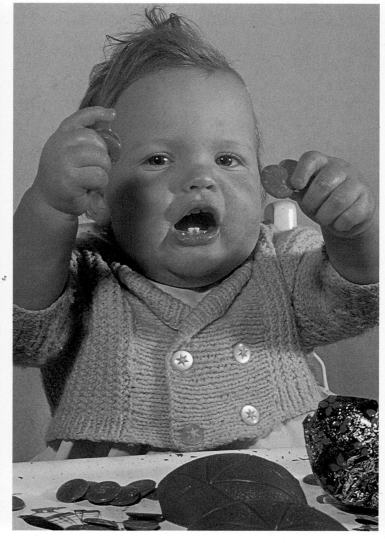

same high standards. Avoid discontinued lines or even special offers that may let you down when in years to come you can't get spare parts – cameras, like all mechanical or electrical appliances, do occasionally break down. Finally, buy the best that you can afford, and don't overlook the possibility of buying second-hand.

A local photographic society or club can be a marvellous source of unbiased advice, so it's well worth attending a few meetings as a potential new member, if only to find out what the experienced members have to say. Unlike the dealer, they are not trying to sell anything. Should you actually join, of course, then the club can provide friends and advice, as well as photographic exercises and the motivation to propel you and your cameras into a visually new world. At the same time, don't fall into the trap of becoming just one more camera freak.

Novice and expert alike can be swayed by colourful packaging and exciting TV and other advertising into adding another 'status symbol' to their equipment but then, when the expected magical result does not work out, they are not so good at seeing that their own inadequacy is to blame, not the camera.

The secret of this shot was to under-expose slightly so that the resulting picture maintained the impression of dawn rather than midday.

WHAT THE CAMERA SEES

A holiday by the sea can teach you the most basic yet most essential lesson in photography – the study of subject depth and perspective. There is the vastness of the glistening sea, the magnificence of the towering cliffs, and the gaily coloured paraphernalia of a holiday resort, all crying out to be captured on film. But while you see everything through two eyes in glorious 3-D technicolour, the camera with only one lens does not, and may even be taking that colourful scene in black and white. It is easy to overlook the fact that the human brain from earliest childhood receives messages not just from the eye, but uses the other senses as well to store up a fund of knowledge about sizes, shapes and substances. Eventually, you almost do not need your eyes to confirm what you already know; the camera, on the other hand, only ever 'sees' what is before it at any given moment.

Basically, your eyes act rather like a zoom lens. Without thinking about it, you can take in at one glance a scene that a camera would require a very wide-angle lens to see, and then, just as unconsciously, you concentrate your vision on a very small part of that scene. However, whether concentrating like a telephoto lens, or inattentive like a wide-angle, you know precisely what you see not only because of that moment of vision, but because the combined experiences of all your senses have proved the scene for you in the past.

You *know*, no matter how distant that mountain or cliff really is, that it is vast and towers to the sky, even though from a distance you don't actually

Right: Only the light from the camp fire illuminates the figures in this picture. An automatic-exposure camera would try to convert this night scene to daylight by over-exposing, whilst flash would have killed the image of the fire's flames. The solution was to use the manual override and reduce the indicated exposure by approximately two stops.

Above: The use of the vacant sentry box at Windsor Castle as a photographic prop makes this picture more than just another portrait. The scene is backlit, but there is a fairly even balance between light and shade so that an automatic camera could have been used.

Right: The figures of the children give a sense of scale and a point of interest to an otherwise undramatic seaside sunset. The exposure has been reduced, but only slightly, and an automatic camera would have coped quite well.

see it that way. Every day you accept thousands of optical illusions without thought, because your brain has already learnt the real truth and told your eyes what you should be seeing.

A very simple example is to look down a long road or railway line and for the moment analyze what you really see. In the near vision the road appears as wide as you *know* it to be, yet no matter how you concentrate your vision it disappears to nothing on the horizon. You don't think about it, because you know that it really is just as wide on the horizon as it is where you are standing. The camera, however, does not know and will portray the scene accordingly – the mountain will only tower magnificently if the camera is close enough for the mountain to dominate the viewfinder.

A popular saying is that the camera *can* lie. It doesn't really, rather it lacks the human brain to correct those illusions which, when seen isolated on a flat print, can be so disappointing. Most photographic problems stem from this natural acceptance of what you *think* you see and blindly expect the camera to interpret, so to be photographically successful you must not only recognize that perspective is a problem, but learn to analyze the intended subject and its surroundings and relate them to your camera's viewfinder.

This one most essential lesson need not take long to learn. Once you accept the principle, it is easy to apply it, yet until you do your snaps will remain snaps. No camera by itself can turn a snap into a picture. In a nutshell, when using a camera you must disbelieve, indeed ignore, what your eyes tell you of a scene; instead, accept and analyze only what you can actually see with a single eye looking through the camera viewfinder. Then ask yourself: 'Does it look right?' If it's a landscape it won't move away, so don't rush, look at that viewfinder image dispassionately as though inspecting a painting or a television image, and be prepared to move the position or angle of the camera.

As you analyze, ask yourself whether things appear to be in the correct proportion, whether there is anything that doesn't seem right or confuses. Above all, remember that your finished picture was there all the time for you to see in the viewfinder. It is impossible to overstate the importance of this lesson. You have to train yourself to acquire visual awareness, and your future success or failure entirely depends on getting this right.

Spending vast sums of money on cameras and ancillary equipment will never make a badly viewed picture better; the rest of this book is in a sense really about how we can make use of our visual awareness to manufacture an end product. Someone else can process and print your film if you don't wish to get involved yourself, but only you can take the picture.

Though visually impressive, Brunel's giant bridge is hardly pretty, so the trick is to construct the picture. A viewpoint was chosen where leaves could be used to camouflage an uninteresting sky-line, while the figures not only illustrate the scale but add that vital touch of red, the most powerful colour in the spectrum.

HOW TO COMPOSE BETTER PICTURES

Much can be learned from looking at other people's photographs and paintings, especially at great works of art of the past. The painter's motivation was (like ours) to capture an image faithfully, and this had very little to do with how many brushes he owned. Simplicity and good perspective were his keynotes, with nothing detracting from the main subject. Painters of course have licence, and certainly the brush can lie, omit some human defect or eyesore on a landscape, but so can you by changing position and using light and shade to its best advantage, and eventually, when you are more experienced, adding filters.

It would be good to think that even family occasions, treated with care and thought, could be works of art, achieving so much more than a snapshot record. After all, in a sense we are all recording for posterity today's social history; so why not make as good a job of it as we can? It is only natural that we should photograph our families, our cars and possessions, and where we have been. Why not try combining some of these elements? Instead of taking yet another shot of Aunt Julie, to bore all but possibly her, use her as a figure in a landscape, even standing by that car. Not only does the resulting picture do three jobs but the figure chosen and the car can give size, proportion and perspective to the landscape; so you step from a snapshot to a picture of interest to all. This way, too, you are controlling and building the picture, like the painter.

Left: Not every picture of people has to be static. By asking the boys to splash an adult friend the photographer gained both expression and movement for this picture. In order to freeze the action a shutter speed of at least 1/250 sec. is needed.

Above: Although standing amidst the beauties of Britain's Lake District, these characters look distinctly bored and amply illustrate how not to take one's holiday snaps.

Right: Though far from perfect, this picture allows the subjects to complement the scene by letting them look at the surroundings and making them more at ease.

Few of us like to be on the other end of a camera, staring back at the lens, whereas if we are placed in a more natural setting and allowed the freedom to look around, we become much more at ease. Remember: it's not necessary always to have your loved ones looking straight at the camera. Children are natural models, unselfconscious and precocious, yet they are usually extremely inquisitive, so if they know they are about to be photographed but are much too interested in your camera, or hamming it up for the photographer, give them time. The best way with children, especially your own, is to let them settle long enough to become used to and bored with the camera. Generally it is best if they can forget you are even there when the picture-taking starts.

With young children it often helps to have plenty of toys and props around to hold their attention, but you in turn must be ready to work quickly to capture those fleeting moments of childish joy, frustration, etc., which are rarely repeated. The garden or park is a marvellous environment for photographing children or animals, giving the photographer room patiently to stalk his or her prey. Keep the subject and pictures as simple and natural as possible, and try to avoid the posed shot.

Don't forget that there is no need to wait for a nice sunny morning; the camera will work at any time, even though you may have to add a flash gun for night pictures, as we shall see later. Should you already have a flash gun, then try not to use it unless absolutely necessary, for if there is any possible photographic light it will generally be softer and much more natural and pleasing than flash. If in doubt, and time allows, try the picture both ways, with and without flash, and don't forget that children asleep make beautiful studies of innocence, a state they rarely display when awake!

Each time you take a picture, keep on analyzing that viewfinder, and follow this up by treating the finished photograph to the same critical inspection. Did you succeed? If not, why not? Self-criticism is rarely wasted. The groundwork put in now will be amply repaid by hours of enjoyment as you and those around you look back on the results. Your ability to analyze will be of far more value than the type of equipment you use. In fact, don't worry about equipment. Just buy film and use it.

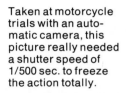

Taken at motorcycle trials with an automatic camera, this picture really needed a shutter speed of 1/500 sec. to freeze the action totally.

The Camera

Although it is perhaps an oversimplification to suggest that the camera is not all that important in the picture-taking process, it is certainly true that the camera is no more than a receptacle, with at one end a lens to arrange the rays of light into an image and a shutter to control that light's duration. Early cameras had neither lenses nor shutters, relying instead on a tiny pinhole in a wooden box to form the image on a glass plate. The operator's hand uncovered and sealed the aperture, admitting light for just the time it was needed.

It took two world wars to bring anything like sophistication to photographic equipment. War made greater demands on the way news was gathered, and this and the added demands of espionage meant that more thought and more money were brought to bear on the technical problems of photography. When peace returned in 1946, the research once again virtually stopped, and although the knowledge was now there, the cost of offering those advances to the ordinary amateur photographer remained too great.

This picture taken during the Boer War is an early example of photojournalism. The subject had to be virtually static so that the photographer with his primitive plate camera and its slow plates could use a time exposure.

Photography and its equipment were set to languish in another technological backwater, but were dramatically rescued by the American space programme. To record those great events in space, in particular that famous 'giant leap for mankind' when Neil Armstrong stepped on to the surface of the Moon, it became necessary to have cameras that could be guaranteed to work in an unknown environment and at incredible variations of temperature, yet at the same time be foolproof in operation whether they were worked by remote control or an untrained operator.

The progress of man in space has cost a vast amount, against which the cost of recording his deeds – while considerable – has been a mere pittance. As a result, enormous developments have taken place, and this time into the automation that ten years later has transformed photography into the world's second most popular hobby. Indeed this momentum has speeded up over the past five years: automatic exposure is becoming almost universal, and we now have sophisticated electronic wizardry in even the most humble and cheap cameras.

The sudden explosion of technology has made not only our previous thinking, but our standards and textbooks, obsolete overnight. Today most cameras are purchased not by the committed amateur photographer, but the casual buyer. This new breed of beginner does not need a mass of technical information before he or she starts taking pictures. Provided he or she learns about basic composition, as explained in the previous chapter, and develops a good eye for a picture, the way is clear for a lifetime of taking acceptable photographs. Failures will be few and far between, and many will be glad to settle for that. However, many of you will want to go on improving, and to find out how better results are achieved.

At that point, despite automation, it becomes necessary to revert to the past and to learn the rudiments of photographic technique and camera design. This way you will be able to understand precisely what is happening, for instance, to the film inside your automatic camera, and will be able to take command, overriding the automatic in favour of manual operation.

There are really only two basic types of camera in popular use: reflex and direct-vision. With a reflex camera the user actually views through the taking lens, via a mirror and complex pentaprism; with direct-vision cameras there is a separate viewfinder and sometimes rangefinder, not unlike a small telescope built into or onto the camera body. These basic systems have literally hundreds of derivatives, different types of shutters, different types of lenses, interchangeable lenses, different-format films, etc., etc., and both systems have their strengths and weaknesses largely because they are born of compromise.

Cameras can be likened to cars, in that to improve significantly the performance of either can raise the unit cost out of all proportion. At the same time there is no more likelihood of finding the universally perfect camera than there is of hitting on the perfect car. To drive five hundred miles a day on a freeway you would surely choose a fast comfortable car, whereas if motoring meant sitting for hours in city traffic jams you would more likely choose something small, economical and easy to park; so it is with cameras.

As a beginner you must ask yourself what you are really likely to do with the camera. If you are likely to want to progress to a wider subject range, it is important to try and establish what that wider range will include. Common sense, coupled with a little knowledge of what is available, will certainly help at the outset, and time spent studying the alternatives now will not be wasted.

The camera must be the cornerstone of your photographic ambitions, and that cornerstone can be difficult, even impossible, to change when a whole system has been built upon it. So let's first consider the merits and disadvantages of the various types.

The Instamatic, the cheapest and most basic camera of all, is still capable of superb results as long as its limitations are recognized and understood.

Shutter speeds

$\frac{1}{2000}$	$\frac{1}{1000}$	$\frac{1}{500}$	$\frac{1}{250}$	$\frac{1}{125}$	$\frac{1}{60}$	$\frac{1}{30}$	$\frac{1}{15}$	$\frac{1}{8}$

face on rotating windmill

side on rotating windmill

running person

This windmill illustrates not only how a faster shutter speed freezes movement but also how movement itself can look faster or slower depending on viewpoint. Looked at face on, the windmill blades soon blur away, whilst viewed side on the image of the blades remains recognizable for much longer.

A racing car traversing our line of vision appears incredibly fast and difficult to watch, yet when viewed head on and coming towards us seemingly takes ages to arrive. We must recognize what is really an optical illusion and change our camera viewpoint when it becomes necessary to freeze the most violent action.

INSTAMATICS AND OTHER BEGINNERS' CAMERAS

This is the simplest development of grandfather's old box camera. It is cheap enough to suit the complete beginner, and foolproof in its cartridge-loading and controls – but not, unfortunately, in its results. If the light is good, and behind you, then you can expect reasonably good results; but when the light is poor so, all too often, are the pictures.

You can find quite sophisticated Instamatics. However, as their cost rises in proportion to their complexity, these cameras with their expensive non-reusable cassettes compare unfavourably with, for example, a bottom-of-the-range full-frame automatic camera.

It remains true, nevertheless, that in ideal conditions you can expect results as good as you will get with a camera of far greater sophistication. The crux, of course, is that not all or even many of your subjects will be taken under ideal conditions, and, what's more, many of them will move! This takes us to the first of our technical problems.

Unless special steps are taken, any movement by the subject during exposure, i.e. while the film is receiving light, will be recorded not as a still image but as a blur. This is why all but the most rudimentary cameras have a range of different shutter speeds for the operator to choose from. If the subject is active, you must choose a speed high enough to stop or isolate any movement. The Instamatic, with its fixed or slow shutter, would completely fail to do this, and owners must restrict the subjects they take to static scenes within the camera's range.

If you have a variable-speed shutter, your range will be far greater (you can even slow its speed to create a deliberate blur). However, it is also important to recognize that by altering the speed or duration of exposure you are also changing the amount of light received by the film. To be able to counteract the latter you need a lens that is capable of transmitting to the film more light, or less, than is actually needed; for while the shutter is used to control subject movement, its effect on exposure has to be corrected.

Moving the shutter speed from, say, 1/125 of a second (1/125 sec.) to 1/500 sec. to freeze rapid action would quarter the amount of light received by the film which would then be underexposed and ruined. To offset this problem the manufacturer provides a variable aperture known as an iris, which acts not unlike a water tap; open it up and more light passes through (or vice versa) to compensate for changes in lighting levels and shutter speeds. Like the shutter speeds the camera lens aperture has an internationally agreed standard measuring scale, so that no matter how large or

Left: To freeze or to blur? These two pictures of similar subjects illustrate how the results may differ even though the exposure to light is identical.
The top picture was taken on a slow shutter speed such as 1/15 sec. with the lens stopped down to f22, whereas the bottom shot had a camera setting of 1/250 sec. at f5.6. Each picture received the same amount of light but for a different duration, and each was panned, i.e. the photographer moved the camera with the subject.
An automatic camera cannot sense that the subject is moving and will therefore probably choose an unsuitable shutter speed, whereas in both illustrations the speeds were deliberately chosen for their effect.

small, or where it was made, any lens or shutter should transmit the same amount of light as any other at a given setting.

As you progress you can use those possible variations to your advantage. Just as shutter speeds control movement, aperture settings control how much of the picture appears in sharp focus. Aperture settings are expressed in a scale of f-numbers, or stops. Although the settings listed below will all transmit exactly the same amount of light to the film, the resulting pictures will differ dramatically between the extremes.

$$1/2000 \text{ sec. at } f2$$
$$1/1000 \text{ sec. at } f2.8$$
$$1/500 \text{ sec. at } f4$$
$$1/250 \text{ sec. at } f5.6$$
$$1/125 \text{ sec. at } f8$$
$$1/60 \text{ sec. at } f11$$
$$1/30 \text{ sec. at } f16$$
$$1/15 \text{ sec. at } f22$$

The first combination will freeze virtually all movement, but the subject will only be sharp in the plane actually focused upon. The last combination will hopelessly blur any movement, but the subject and its surroundings will appear sharp almost as far as the eye can see.

Viewfinder frame

Left: Carefully framed and taken head on, this picture of American motorcycle racer Pat Hennen was in practice easier to take and freeze than the side-on shot of the water skier on the opposite page. Anticipating the shot, the photographer focused on the ground at the bend, lining up the two halves of the central circle in the viewfinder frame, as shown, and adjusting until the outer circle became clear. Having focused, he then moved his camera to frame the rider, and took the shot at the moment when he was in perfect focus. With the subject head on and slowing up at the bend, a very fast shutter speed was not necessary.

Later on we will explore the possibilities of variable shutter speeds/aperture settings in greater detail. For now, the important thing to remember is: when you choose a camera, make sure it has this variable facility. Although you can get a manual override with some automatic cameras, not all are equipped with it. But if you don't have it, you will eventually find yourself severely limited. The simple message is: do not buy a camera that is exclusively automatic unless it is intended only as a second camera, to back up a more versatile instrument.

AUTOMATIC CAMERAS

Automation comes in two forms: total or programmed, and priority. With total automation, the camera chooses both the shutter speed and the aperture. This method is fine when you are a complete beginner; most people are delighted to achieve an immediate 90% success rate on landscapes and static subjects. The disadvantages begin to show either when movement is introduced or you want to isolate just one part of the subject from a confused background. The camera can't tell what you want, though; it will treat every aspect of the subject in the same way, and choose an average shutter speed/aperture combination. As long as the camera has a complete manual override facility, then these problems need only be temporary, and easily solved as soon as you have mastered the business of shutter/aperture combinations.

The other and by and large better form of automation – the priority type – allows the user to choose one half of the possible combination. In other words, you choose a shutter speed and then, to provide the film with enough light, the camera automatically sets the correct aperture to go with it (or vice versa). This method gives everyone greater scope. Even the beginner can benefit from it, one way being to leave the shutter speed permanently on one setting, say 1/125 sec., which is adequate for most subjects. When special occasions arise, e.g. for recording rapid movement, the camera can be reset to a higher speed and left to do the rest automatically.

Better still, though, is *full* manual choice. Once you have sufficient experience, and really understand your camera, there will be many times when you will want to contrive pictures in extreme lighting conditions, sunsets and snow scenes for instance, with which automation cannot cope.

The main point to remember about automation is that the camera, no matter how sophisticated, cannot think for you. Its exposure-reading system has been set by the manufacturer to deal with all *average* subjects, and you must take care of the rest.

This Canon camera has fully automatic exposure setting as well as even focusing and flash. Unfortunately the user cannot move the flash gun away from the camera so flash photographs taken with it will show shadows and red eyes.
Another disadvantage is that the user cannot choose or even know what shutter speed/ aperture combination this camera is set at, so it is really for the very beginner or for use as a second camera restricted to photographing static subjects.

FULL-FRAME FIXED-LENS AUTOMATICS

This is the camera of the masses. Used by pro and amateur alike, it has the real advantage of using normal 35-mm film, which is standard anywhere in the world and available in lengths of 12, 20 or 36 exposures. And although it is derived from the original box camera, employs a separate viewfinder rather than seeing through the taking lens, and is limited to one permanently-fixed focal-length lens, this type of camera is adequate for all but the most advanced or specific needs.

The actual specification will be determined by the price you pay. A wide-aperture light-collecting lens such as an f1.9 obviously costs much more than a simpler, smaller f3.5, yet the former considerably expands the range of the camera. Other choices are: having full automation or fully manual operation on the flick of a switch; delayed-action devices so that you can set the camera and then get into your own picture, and a full range of variable shutter speeds. These all cost money, too, and you must be sure you know what you are looking for.

Earlier we likened cameras to cars, each model having its particular strengths and weaknesses. Undoubtedly the major advantages of the fixed-lens full-frame automatics are their cost, weight and size. Added to these are a lens with a wider-than-usual angle of acceptance, and some flash-lighting benefits which we shall investigate later.

Olympus's OM-1 (manual) and OM-2 (automatic or manual) are amongst the very best cameras to grow up and learn with. The OM-2 allows the user automation or full manual override and is therefore suitable for raw beginner and expert alike.

Bulk and weight can be of great importance to the walker, the climber and the cyclist, while for everyday use the camera that fits in a briefcase or handbag may seem an attractive proposition. What is more, the wider-than-usual lens can be a boon for indoor photography and for landscapes.

Against these advantages you need to bear in mind that this camera's separate viewfinder can never be accurate, only approximating to what the lens can see. Also, not only can the lens not be changed for, say, a telephoto to bring distant objects closer, its wider angle would then be a disadvantage. Finally, although filters and close-up lenses can be used on this type of camera, their effects can only be guessed at, and extreme close-ups are impossible owing to the limited focusing range of the fixed lens.

SINGLE-LENS REFLEX CAMERAS (SLR)

At one time almost exclusively the professional's camera, and conservatively manual in its construction and operation, the SLR is now much more widely used. Today's SLRs are offered with all forms of automation and with full manual override, and while they tend to be more expensive than the simpler full-frame direct-vision cameras, the SLRs come closest to the ideal of the all-round camera. Internally, whether designed for roll film or 35 mm, they are the most advanced cameras on the market.

The SLR has two advantages. The lenses are interchangeable, and the photographer can view, compose and focus the subject, with near-total accuracy, through the actual taking lens. On its own the SLR has little more potential than the direct-vision camera, but with extra lenses and filters it becomes a versatile tool that can produce results of the highest quality, and do so under the most varied conditions. Using it, you can separate yourself from the scenery as the eye sees it, and really compose your picture on the camera's screen, which you look at like a miniature TV.

The camera has a pentaprism which, via a mirror placed at 45 degrees between lens and film, looks out through the actual taking lens. Through it you can accurately gauge the effects of filters – which can considerably enrich both black-and-white and colour photography – of close-up lenses and even of macro and micro photography.

There are nevertheless disadvantages, quite apart from cost. SLRs are bulky and often heavy, especially in roll-film format, and there is a slight delay between when you thought you took the picture and when you actually took it. The reason for this lies in the SLR's 45-degree mirror that bends the rays of light passing through the lens up to the pentaprism, and finally to the eyepiece on top of the camera.

Mamiya's 645 is one of the best roll-film single-lens reflex cameras, having an eye-level viewing capacity and even automatic exposure by means of an extra clip-on through-the-lens metering pentaprism.

With SLR cameras there is a delay between the moment the shutter is pressed and the moment when the picture is actually taken. During this time the viewing mirror has to move out of the way of the lens, which must itself stop down to its predetermined aperture. The larger the camera the greater this delay and the more difficult it becomes to time action shots such as this where one wants to keep the ball in the picture.

When you take a picture this mirror, placed between the lens and the film, has to pivot upwards to serve a double function. Firstly it has to allow the light access to the film when the shutter opens, and secondly it has to mask the pentaprism so that light does not enter the camera from both ends via the eyepiece. This action can take several milliseconds, during which time the shutter cannot begin to do its job. Meanwhile your subject may still be moving and, what's more, vision through the viewfinder is lost by the mirror until the exposure process has ended and the mirror drops down again, ready for the next frame.

With sporting subjects, and some scientific ones, this delay can be a major snag. Indeed, at any time when movement is both rapid and sudden there is a good chance that the SLR will miss it; the larger the camera format, the greater this delay will be, owing to the greater distance the mirror and shutter must travel.

TWIN-LENS REFLEX CAMERAS (TLR)

Exclusively a roll-film camera rather than a 35-mm, the TLR is a compromise between the two basic types of camera. It is virtually two box cameras coupled together, each with its own lens.

One half is a viewing and focusing system, and as such does not need a shutter or film compartment. The other, which actually moves with it, takes the picture which the photographer has composed and focused through the first lens. The twin-lens reflex camera is really outdated today, ousted by the SLR roll-film camera.

This twin-lens reflex, the Mamiya C330, is unique among TLRs in that the lens panels can be interchanged, allowing wide-angle or telephoto lenses to be fitted. Its Achilles heel is that the top viewing lens does not see precisely the same field of view as the taking lens and so some guesswork is needed to reduce parallax error.

Focal plane shutter

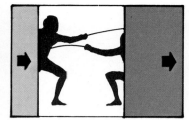

Top: As the focal-plane shutter's blind traverses the film and the image being reflected on to it by the lens, so it uncovers and re-covers that image. The fencers illustrated are moving throughout but that movement can only be recorded on film whilst that area of film is momentarily unveiled. This is why the focal-plane shutter is more efficient at freezing movement, for it is not the overall exposure duration that is important but the sectional duration.

Left: Some shutters traverse comparatively slowly, with a narrow slit for the fast speeds (1 and 4) and a larger slit for slow, whilst all must have at least one speed setting at which the slit is wide enough to uncover the whole film for flash use (3). Others achieve much the same result by increasing the slit width (2–5), but traversing that slit much more quickly. In practice the latter is better both for flash and for freezing motion.

Focal plane shutter, exposure time

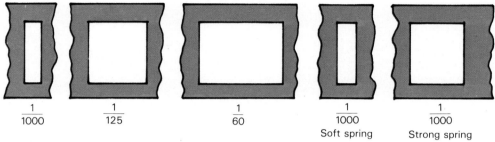

$\frac{1}{1000}$ $\frac{1}{125}$ $\frac{1}{60}$ $\frac{1}{1000}$ Soft spring $\frac{1}{1000}$ Strong spring

Focal plane shutter

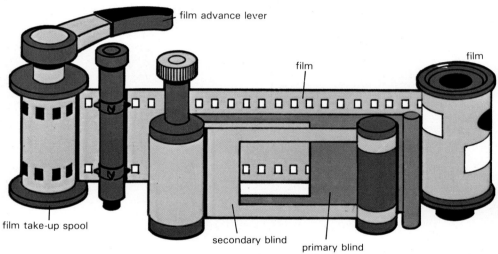

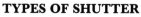

Above: Schematic drawing of the focal-plane shutter in position in front of the film. Note that there are in fact two blinds and that the slit width and therefore the shutter speeds are changed by moving the position of one blind in relation to the other so as to vary the slit width.

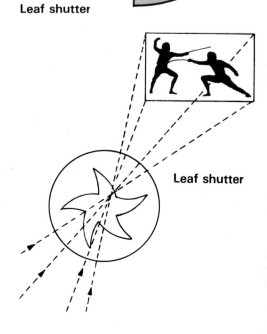

Leaf shutter

Leaf shutter

POLAROID OR INSTANT-PICTURE CAMERAS

Not for the serious photographer, though deserving of mention, these cameras are fixed-lens automatic cameras with a fairly large film format, and deliver a positive print little more than seconds after exposure. The Polaroid's major limitations are the bulk of the camera and the expense of the film. The bulk tends to limit usage to around the home, and the expense to infrequent use. Furthermore, since few models deliver a negative it is both difficult and expensive to obtain extra prints.

TYPES OF SHUTTER

All modern 35-mm SLR cameras and most roll-film versions use a *focal-plane* shutter positioned at the rear of the camera and in close proximity to the film. This term, though adopted to describe a shutter type, really means the point at which the lens brings its rays of light together to form the image. An obvious advantage of so placing the shutter is that when not in use it totally covers the film, forming a light-tight compartment. This allows the camera's lens to be removed and changed without any 'fogging' of the film through leakage.

The twin-lens reflex cameras employ a *leaf* or *compur* shutter built into each taking lens. Some roll-film SLRs have both front (compur) and rear (focal-plane) shutters fitted, though these are mainly for professional applications. Interchangeable-lens cameras, with only a blade-type of front shutter, must also have a simple additional blind or door so that, before the lens is changed, the film area is sealed off from light.

You need to know how the two types of shutter do their job in order to understand the definite advantages and disadvantages of each, which can have a considerable bearing on which camera you choose.

The focal-plane shutter is a cloth or metal-foil blind not unlike a roller curtain, which has cut into it a series of slits of varying widths, and the whole assembly is tensioned by springs when the camera is wound on. When the operator chooses a fast shutter speed, he or she is in fact selecting a very narrow slit, while a slow speed would be one of the largest or longest slits. When the shutter is pressed, the slit traverses the film and light is admitted.

The diagrams show that the short-exposure narrow slit uncovers and then re-covers the film in segments as it passes. If the subject moves at some other moment in the overall exposure, this cannot be recorded on that area of film already re-covered, even though the shutter is still working. Instead of blurring, this additional movement will be converted into a slight distortion, the moving object within the picture being foreshortened if its travel is in the opposite direction to the shutterblind, and lengthened if both are travelling in the same direction. To reduce this effect and increase shutter efficiency in oblong-format cameras, many manufacturers place the shutter to move across the shortest part of the frame, i.e. from top to bottom rather than across.

The major limitation of this type of shutter design is with flash photography. Although the flash duration is extremely short, the focal-plane shutter, while uncovering and re-covering each segment of the film at its set speed, say 1/1000 sec., can actually take much longer to traverse the whole frame. This means that only one segment receives the flash's light, which appears on the negative or transparency as a bright bar across the frame, not unlike a TV picture with horizontal-hold problems.

Flash can therefore only be used at the lowest speeds on this type of shutter, or in other words where the slit is long enough at one stage in its movement to uncover the whole frame area – only then can the flash fire to give a complete picture (usually at about 1/60 sec.). With an enforced low shutter speed of 1/60 sec. or slower, and a probable flash duration somewhere in the region of 1/5000 sec., there is therefore considerable risk of both blurring and double images on the finished picture. This is the one major problem area of the focal-plane shutter, and also the reason why some professionals' cameras incorporate an additional compur shutter more suited to flash photography. This is usually built into the actual taking lens.

The compur shutter comprises a number of blades to form an iris, not unlike the lens aperture control. The shutter blades are coupled to a powerful spring which, when the shutter is pressed, makes the blades open and close to admit light. In action it is like a flower opening and closing, the petals or blades uncovering the whole lens area each time a picture is taken. This also allows flash to be used no matter what the shutter speed may be.

There are two main disadvantages. Firstly, the compur shutter is built into the lens, which means that with an interchangeable-lens camera a costly shutter must be bought with each additional lens. Secondly, because it must uncover the whole field for the entire duration of each exposure, its ability to stop movement is greatly reduced.

In simple terms, the focal-plane shutter is superior in every way except for flash photography, and your decision which to buy must be made entirely on the basis of how you expect to use your camera.

Before leaving the subject of the basic camera, one word of warning, especially to the 35-mm user or the infrequent photographer, no matter how experienced. Do read the maker's instruction book, and as far as possible memorize the salient points; above all, take special care with loading. More films are wasted and pictures lost in the loading process than for any other reason. Common mistakes are: reloading an already used film; forgetting to load, and forgetting whether the camera is still loaded. Everyone seems to suffer from these problems, but you can reduce your failures by fostering a few simple habits.

1 When loading a 35-mm camera, fire three blank frames and at the same time watch the re-wind crank lever to check that it is turning round. If the crank turns all is well, but if it does not then the film isn't going through the camera. It is such a simple thing to overlook but it often happens for mechanical reasons: the sprocket holes rip on the single film tongue or starter, and so defeat you even before you've begun.

2 To avoid re-using an already exposed film, never wind the film right back into the cassette but leave a few inches of film out; after all, they were only those three blank frames anyway.

3 Tear off the starter tongue so that you cannot accidentally re-load that film. This has the added advantage that the film helps to seal the cassette light trap and stops accidental fogging.

4 If in doubt whether the 35-mm camera is already loaded, don't open the camera back but instead take up the slack on the re-wind lever *without* pressing the re-wind button. If it becomes tense the camera is loaded, if it remains free it's not.

5 When coming to the end of the film, the wind-on lever will suddenly stiffen, perhaps even in mid-stroke. It is essential that it is not forced, which could damage both camera and film, possibly tearing the film out of its cassette; you would then need a dark room to unload.

Most instruction books for 35-mm cameras illustrate the loading operation as below, with the film engaged into the take-up spool but not yet engaged on the top drive sprocket. To be sure that the film is actually transported through the camera it is *vital* that before the camera back is closed the film is wound a little further and engaged on *both* sprockets to avoid the danger of ripping.

Below: Most SLR cameras are supplied with a split-image focusing prism built into the viewing screen (left), whilst some more sophisticated cameras provide the better microprism focusing screen (centre). Unfortunately both systems often black out completely when the camera is fitted with either wide-angle or telephoto lenses, especially those of a lower maximum aperture than the normal standard lens. Where a choice is available or viewfinder screens can be interchanged a plane ground centre spot which does not black out (right) is to be preferred.

About Lenses

The nucleus of any camera, enlarger or projector system is its optic or lens. It *must* be good, for we depend on it to reproduce the subject faithfully and with detail and clarity. It must be able to do its job no matter how poor the light, and no matter what the climatic conditions.

The wise buyer will want to test any lens he is thinking of buying. It could well be worthwhile running through a roll of film on the dealer's premises, for this could even determine the choice of the camera itself, especially if it is to be a fixed-lens instrument. And if cost is an important factor, it is better to do without a few camera facilities than to skimp on the quality of the lens.

The duty of the optic is to collect all the rays of light bouncing off the subject, and to rearrange and reduce them to the comparatively tiny size of the film. At the same time it must keep out reflections and stray light coming from beyond its own field of vision. Most important of all, if for a moment we imagine a potential landscape scene, it must transform a view filled with near and distant objects into a faithful single-dimensional version on flat film. To achieve this, many different elements, or lenses within the lens, are needed, and when we talk about 'the lens' we often really mean something with as many as 22 different components.

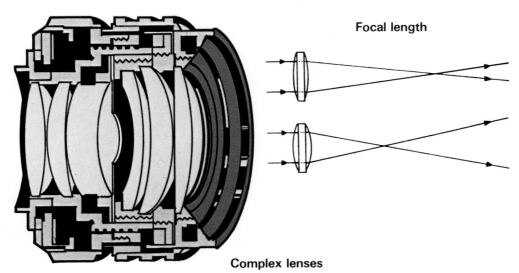

Focal length

Complex lenses

A typical complex multi-element standard lens for an SLR camera.

Glass elements of different thicknesses and with greater or lesser radii obviously bend light at different angles and therefore alter the lens's focal length.

Early lens designers were consistently frustrated in their desire to produce the perfect optic because they could not find suitable earth glasses to achieve the effects they wanted. Lens design proceeded by trial and error, and it often took years to perfect a particular type. Today, with the aid of computers and man-made glasses such as fluorite grown from crystals, the advances in optical design have been just as great as the camera revolution brought about by electronics and automation. The effect of these optical advances, introducing glass elements to bend light in ways previously thought impossible, has been to make the modern camera, almost regardless of price, far superior to that of a generation ago.

Early single-element lenses suffered in two main ways. Firstly, their image was projected in a curved plane – and camera designers actually tried curving the surface of the film to meet the lens's image. Secondly, their designers understood little of what we now know to be chromatic or colour aberration.

Put simply, if any lens element is divided into sections you see it as a series of prisms and, as any student of physics will know, prisms split the white light that we see into the three primary colours of red, green and blue-

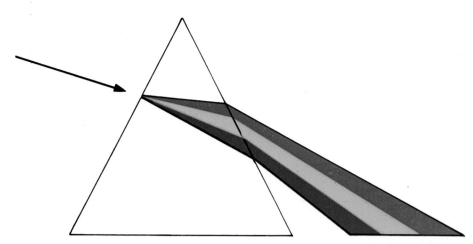

Right: When light passes through glass it is bent or refracted. If that glass also happens to be a prism then the white light is not only bent but also split up into the three primary colours, red, green and blue-violet.

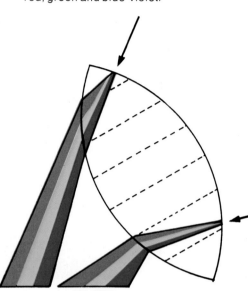

Above: A lens element is really like a collection of prisms joined together and the transmitted light will be bent differently depending on the thickness of that lens or prism. Camera lenses have more than one element so that they can bend the rays of light back together at the film plane.

Above right and right: Although the image size is much the same in these two pictures the perspective is totally different. The top picture was taken with a 24-mm wide-angle lens and the lower with a 200-mm telephoto. To retain the image size the photographer moved his position, and the changes of background and perspective are entirely due to the different camera positions, not to the variation between the focal lengths of the two lenses.

violet. Whether or not you are using colour film, you are most certainly photographing coloured objects which our simple lens has refracted or split from one colour image into three, and those rays have to be bent back to a single colour as the light emerges from the other side of the lens and before it reaches the film.

Perhaps it is as well that colour photography took almost 70 years to invent after Fox-Talbot and his day. He would probably have been staggered to find his images fringed by the primary colours because the lenses available in those days could not bend the rays of light back together.

There are two indisputable laws of the lens. The first is that perspective is entirely a product of viewpoint, the second that depth of field, i.e. that amount in acceptably sharp focus on either side of the image being focused upon, is dependent on the focal length of the lens and its aperture setting.

An unfortunate yet popular photographic myth has it that merely by changing the focal length of the lens to a longer or shorter one, you change the subject's perspective. You do not. Only by changing your distance from the subject does perspective alter. (However, if you were to change both lens and distance, then you could appear to make mountains into molehills and tots into giants – truly making the camera lie, but by choice rather than accident.)

Depth of field is controllable either by varying lens lengths or apertures, for any lens has some residual depth of field. (Lenses also have, incidentally, some residual depth of focus, i.e. the amount of acceptably sharp focus on either side of the film plane, which helps to counteract any bowing of the film.)

To use either perspective or depth the photographer must fully understand each phenomenon. When combined, they become the greatest assets in the search for and the making of good pictures.

PERSPECTIVE

Imagine that you are photographing a distant landscape from a static position, and that you have available to you a range of lenses from the longest telephoto to the shortest wide-angle. Obviously, if you took a picture with each, the photographs would appear dramatically different. The ultra-wide-angle lens would reproduce an area greater even than your eyes could accept without turning your head sideways, while the telephoto would act as a binocular, bringing closer a remote and distant part of the scene.

If the subject were a distant mountain range, in the first instance it would appear tiny and insignificant, and in the second dramatic and dominating. This might mislead you into thinking that the perspective had changed, whereas in fact all that has altered is the degree of enlargement. You have merely pulled up or enlarged a portion of the scene, and close scrutiny of the centre of the print or transparency taken on the ultra-wide-angle would confirm that it was in identical proportion or perspective to the whole of the picture taken on the telephoto.

If, using the same extremes of lenses, you then move nearer to your subject, those lenses will again produce identical perspectives to each other, but both will have changed in perspective from the first example. It sounds complicated but you can easily demonstrate it to yourself with a camera and lens, and without having to take any pictures.

Get a friend to stand a few metres in front of a large object such as a house or car, while you look carefully through the viewfinder from a distance of some 15 or 18 metres (50 or 60 feet). The person and house will both appear to be as they should be, i.e. in correct proportion. Now move the camera closer, but without altering the subject's position in relation to the house, and look again.

This time the figure in the viewfinder will appear to be taller than the house. To exaggerate the point, ask him or her to stretch a hand out towards the camera and you will find that the outstretched hand becomes even larger than the figure or house. Changing to a wide-angle would drastically increase this distortion, not because the lens itself has a bearing on perspective, but because it is so wide and gives an apparently smaller picture, forcing the operator to move closer to retain the same image size. Conversely, with a telephoto you would have to move the camera position much further away to get the figure in at all; once again, because the camera position has had to be moved, the perspective has dramatically changed.

The real value of having lenses of differing focal length is not merely to get more or less in – after all, there are few subjects for which we can't do that ourselves, by moving closer or further away. No, the real value is to be able to cheat or alter perspective.

DEPTH OF FIELD

When a lens is focused on a specific object or distance, the operator still has a certain amount of latitude to either side of that point. This surrounding sharp area always falls in two parts. The front part, roughly one-third of the area, lies before the actual focal point, and the second part, about two-thirds of the area, lies behind it. Thus, for example, if our lens at a given

Above: Using an extreme (17-mm) wide-angle lens to emphasize the distortion of perspective.

Below: These simple illustrations show how a photographer can alter perspective by changing both viewpoint and lens.
1. Telephoto from a long distance away.
2. Normal lens from a normal distance.
3. Wide-angle lens from close up.

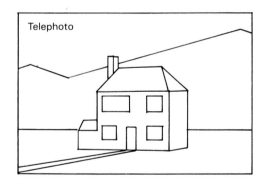

Telephoto

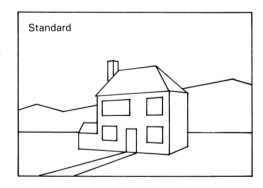

Standard

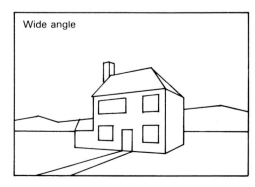

Wide angle

setting was capable of 3 metres' total depth when set at 30 metres, then everything between 29 metres and 32 metres would also appear to be in sharp focus.

Precisely how much depth a lens can give depends on its focal length, and the aperture it is set at. The shortest lens, set at the smallest aperture and focused on the maximum distance, would give the greatest depth of field. The question of distance is relative, for depths are assessed in percentages; a lens with a focal length and aperture setting aimed to give, say, 30% depth would do so no matter what the distance set.

It follows that the percentage distance, when measured on a subject focused upon at 1,000 metres, would be vastly greater than when focused on at 10 metres. Since depth increases as focal length decreases, it also follows that if you were to combine a wide-angle lens, having the maximum possible depth of field potential, with the smallest stop or aperture, then enormous depth would be available.

You can use this knowledge to your advantage, for instance by choosing an ultra-wide-angle lens such as a 17-mm fitted to a 35-mm camera. This will give you everything in sharp focus from just in front of the camera to as far as the eye can see, and almost obviates the need to focus. Alternatively, by choosing a long or telephoto lens, deliberately set at maximum or wide aperture, you can reduce that depth to inches to isolate just one part of the picture. These are extreme examples between which, by varying lenses and aperture settings (at the expense of shutter speed), you can totally change the visual concept of any picture.

Naturally, you need to know just how much depth of field your lenses are capable of at any given focused distance or aperture setting. In fact the manufacturer provides an approximate depth-of-field scale by engraving on the focusing ring a series of additional marks, on either side of the infinity

These diagrams illustrate how depth of field changes according to the distance between lens and subject. Each camera has the same lens, set at the same f stop, but the distance from the subject varies. Depth of field is a percentage of this distance and is therefore narrowest where the distance is 1 metre (left) and increases where it is 3 metres (centre) or 30 metres (right).

Depth of field also increases with shorter lenses and with smaller apertures and decreases with longer lenses and with larger apertures, so that it can be controlled by changing the combination of these. The depth-of-field scale engraved on each lens will provide useful guidelines.

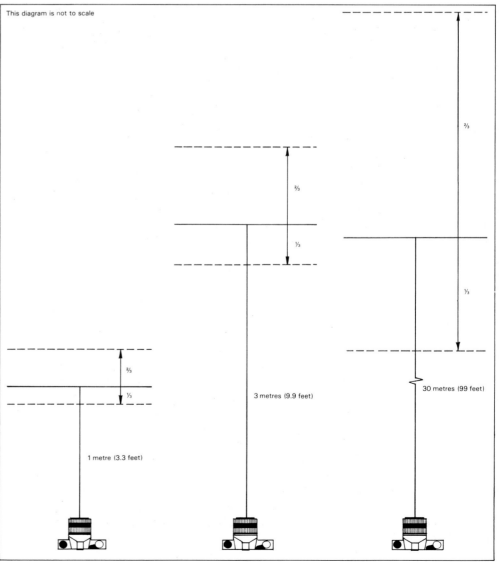

This diagram is not to scale

1 metre (3.3 feet)

3 metres (9.9 feet)

30 metres (99 feet)

Depth of field

By using an ultra-wide-angle lens to give maximum depth of field the photographer has here been able to keep the flowers only inches away and the mountain in sharp focus. The change in perspective has, however, made the mountain appear smaller.

mark (∞) ; these show, for each aperture setting, how much of your subject will still be in sharp focus on either side of the point focused upon. By using this scale you can then decide not only the distance at which you first need good definition, but also, as with a conflicting background, at which point you would like this definition to end.

The technique is simple : you merely focus on the first point that you wish to be sharp and read off the distance on the lens-focusing scale, repeat the exercise on the furthest subject point needing similarly sharp definition, and the distance between those two objects is the depth you require.

Let's go a stage further and imagine that you have a scene with two such points, each some distance from each other, but the immediate foreground or distant background threatens to intrude on and possibly spoil your picture. The next step is to look at the depth-of-field scale on the lens and move it to a setting which, combined with the aperture scale, would encompass those nearest and furthest points, and alter your focused distance to match. In other words, neither of your chief subjects is actually focused on ; the real point of focus set on the lens lies somewhere between the two, at the mid-point in the depth of field.

This process of viewing and focusing with a through-the-lens reflex camera, where you actually see the effect of your focusing on the camera's viewing screen, can be somewhat confusing in that you appear to be moving your lens to a position where none of the items you want in sharp focus looks to be so on the screen. In practice, though, when you are viewing the lens is set at full aperture, so that the image is at its brightest and its depth at a minimum, to make visual focusing easy. However, when the picture is actually taken the viewing lens stops itself down to the predetermined taking aperture, at which point the depth increases as the aperture decreases – something you could not see while viewing wide-open.

To counteract this problem, most reflex cameras have what is known as a stop-down button which closes the iris to the taking setting without actually

The golf ball in this picture appears to be larger than Peter Oosterhuis's head. This is the price the photographer had to pay in terms of perspective in order to achieve this ultra-wide-angle picture.

8mm

18mm

35mm

50mm

85mm

135mm

100°

63°

47°

29°

180°

18

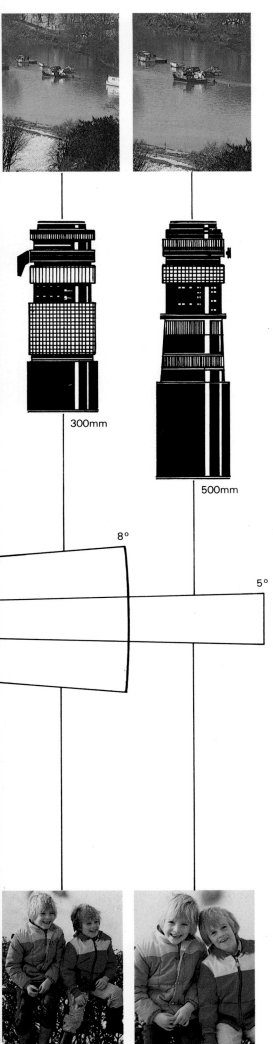

300mm

500mm

8°

5°

needing to take a picture, so that the operator can study just how much depth is available. The problem then is that the viewing image is so dark that depth is almost impossible to judge. For this reason, people with reflex cameras tend to overlook the fact that they can move or change their depth of field to suit their subject. Once they have focused through the lens and achieved a sharp image, it seems only natural to leave things as they are.

It is unfortunate that the traditional way of buying a camera is with a lens already fitted. Usually it is known as the 'standard' lens, but with a lot of SLRs it is inappropriate and unusable. The reason is that when the first SLRs were designed, the manufacturers needed a little more space to accommodate the mirror box, and so moved the lens further away, adopting a standard focal length of 50 mm or even 55 mm. This is appreciably longer than the lens with a 35-mm focal length which, fitted to a 35-mm camera, delivers the nearest parallel to what we actually see.

The overall effect of the standard SLR lens is to give an artificial perspective to the subject, which makes it all the harder to make an accurate interpretation when viewing through the camera.

A strong argument exists for buying an interchangeable-lens camera *without* the standard lens, and instead choose a shorter focal lens such as the 35-mm, from within that same manufacturer's range. Most professionals and experienced amateurs prefer a minimum combination of two lenses, one slightly wider than standard and the other slightly longer. From there they add lenses of more extreme lengths from ultra-wide angles to enormous telephotos, enabling themselves to control and exploit both perspective and depth.

One final point: look after your lens. It is a valuable piece of equipment and should always be covered when not in use. Sand, rain, cheap lens-cleaning tissues and even greasy fingerprints can permanently damage a lens. Instead of an ordinary cover, try fitting a filter. These can be far more effective. Either an ultra violet (UV) or a skylight (Wratten 1A) filter would be best, since these filter out ultra-violet or blue light which the eye does not see. They cost little and are easily replaced.

Left: Each sequence of photographs accompanying this lens chart tells a different story. The pictures in the top row were each taken with the lenses indicated and from an identical viewpoint. Close examination will reveal that the perspective does not change. However, when the same lenses were moved nearer to the subject, as in the bottom row of photographs, the perspective was altered as the focal lengths shortened.

Above: A semi-fisheye picture of the Moscow Olympic cycling where the photographer has used this lens's inherent distortion to his own advantage.

31

Choosing and Understanding Film

To the beginner the vast range of film types, sizes and speeds, black-and-white and colour, must be totally bewildering, but there is one basic fact that everyone can remember – there is no need to throw money away. The faster the film, the worse the overall qualities of grain and definition will be, so the first lesson is not to use high-speed film needlessly. After that, the choice of make is largely a personal one – so buy what suits you.

WHAT FILMS ARE MADE OF

Films are an emulsional mixture of silver halide granules which chemically react to light; they are mixed in a solution of gelatine and coated onto celluloid to make them flexible for passing through the camera. Black-and-white films have one coating or layer while colour films have three, one for each of the primary colours. Each layer has a built-in filter to cut out all but its own colour, so that really there are three images sandwiched together (this is the reason why colour films are so much thicker).

Every film has a speed or figure of measurement to show how it reacts to light. The speed value is printed on the film carton before the letters ASA, which is the internationally agreed measuring standard. To make an emulsion faster, the manufacturer adds more and larger silver halide grains; these, when clumped together, give the characteristic graininess of high-speed films.

The speed of a film represents the threshold or point at which light becomes strong enough to record an image. The quoted figure is really an average setting, sufficient to cope with ordinary subjects in which both light and shade are featured. To measure light, use either the camera's built-in exposure meter, or a separate hand-held meter which tells you how much light is available; you then set that against the speed of the film in use.

PRINTS AND TRANSPARENCIES

There are two different types of colour and black-and-white films, negative and positive. The latter is also known as reversal film. Negative films, as the name implies, produce a reversed image; with black-and-white film, what was white in the subject becomes black on the film, and vice versa. Colour negative films make a similar transition, the primary colours of light being reversed to their opposites. Photographic printing papers also work on the same principle; they are simply negative emulsions coated onto paper.

To obtain a print from the negative, the whole camera process is reversed by placing the negative in an enlarger, which is simply a camera with the light source behind it rather than in front, and projecting the negative image

Fast films have a thicker light-sensitive emulsion coating than slow films and also more of the large grains. Unfortunately light tends to bounce back off the celluloid onto which this emulsion is coated, and then this bounced light scatters within the emulsion and diffuses the potential image definition. The thicker the emulsion the greater this definition loss so that fast films tend to be less sharp and of course more grainy.

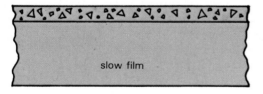

slow film

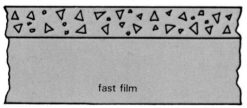

fast film

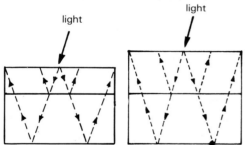

Right: Most colour films have three emulsion layers, each with a colour filter beneath and all coated onto the common celluloid base. With transparency film the first layer (blue) reacts to one third of the spectrum and reverses to make a yellow image. The next layer (green-sensitive) similarly reverses to provide a magenta image, whilst the final (red) layer forms into cyan (blue-green).

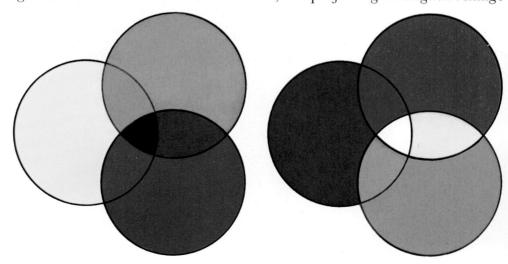

A typical contact print, made by printing strips of black-and-white roll-film negatives in face contact with light-sensitive paper. This serves as a file print from which to choose pictures suitable for enlargement.

onto photographic printing paper. The projected image records on exactly the same type of emulsion, and the colours are once again reversed to produce a positive print; the paper is then processed or stabilized.

Reversal films are more complex to process because, to give a positive image or transparency without enlargement or projection, the film has to have an extra exposure to light during processing, to reverse its image.

When buying film, the basic choice is between ending up with prints that can easily be shown around, or transparencies which need to be projected. Another point to consider is whether you are likely, even in the distant future, to process and print your own results.

Prints from negative film can of course be carried around in a wallet or pocket or framed and hung on the wall, whereas the transparency needs to be projected onto a screen or looked at through a viewer, and as such is obviously less easy to view in ideal conditions than a print. However, you also have to consider the quality of the end-result.

Print films, owing to the double process that ends in a paper print, are severely limited in their contrast acceptance range. To reach the print stage, the original brilliant tones have to be drastically reduced, often spoiling much of the subject's initial appeal. Transparencies, on the other hand, with one process only and a translucent image rather than a reflected one, will retain far more contrast, tones and detail. This is the reason, for example, why the colour pictures published in books are taken off transparencies rather than prints. Add to this the fact that it is a simple matter to have a print taken off a transparency, which is done by using reversal paper, and you can have the best of both worlds. This in fact makes a strong case for the transparency.

Most of the other decisions you make will depend on who does the processing. If, for example, your negative film is sent away for developing and printing, then each frame, or certainly each acceptable frame, will be enlarged. This can be a costly and wasteful business, especially in colour and on occasions when you have taken several similar shots and only want one print of the best.

'Free film' offers, with cheap processing, are nothing more than a sales gimmick that takes advantage of the customer. The film is not in reality free, nor is the processing cheap. What is happening is that the processing house is ensuring that it not only retains your business by supplying the next film, but that every possible shot is printed.

The mud-splattered rugby players (top) were captured on film under near impossible lighting conditions which dictated that the fastest type of film be used, whereas the shot of the Olympic gymnast (above) was taken on much slower film indoors. The author used high contrast *slow* film to capture Leonard Stock winning the Lake Placid Olympic Downhill Skiing Gold Medal (right). The choice of film was dictated by poor light conditions with low contrast

If you use transparencies, though, you can first view the entire processed roll, and only then, preferably after projection, decide which transparencies you want to have printed. This cuts out wastage and saves you money.

The best solution, if you are using negative or print film, is to have contact prints made in the first place, rather than enlargements. You can then select for enlargement only those negatives which are aesthetically pleasing and portray what you had hoped for, and which you will also have checked for sharpness with a magnifying glass.

LIGHT CONDITIONS

The subject and its lighting will determine whether a fast or slow film is required, and, with colour-reversal films, whether it should be of an artificial or daylight type. Remember: if you choose a faster film than you really need, you are throwing away the chance of good definition in exchange for decreased contrast and tone range, and increased graininess.

Even in dull conditions you do not need a fast film for the vast majority of outdoor subjects. The slower the film, the finer the grain and the greater the contrast and tone range, with maximum contrast *when it is most needed*. When you are working in poor light, the subject becomes less than sparkling, and you really need that contrast. This, together with a fine tone range, is what will lift the subject out of its temporary drabness.

Naturally, if you have to photograph an action subject by available light indoors, or under conditions such as floodlights, then your options are removed and you must accept the limitations on quality and use a film with a speed or light-gathering power commensurate with the scene. Colour reversal films are specifically balanced accurately to record either daylight or tungsten artificial light, but not both; this factor does not greatly affect negative colour or black-and-white film. With the former you can correct the colour balance in the enlarger, and since colour in the latter will be reduced to blacks, greys and whites anyway, the light source is of little consequence.

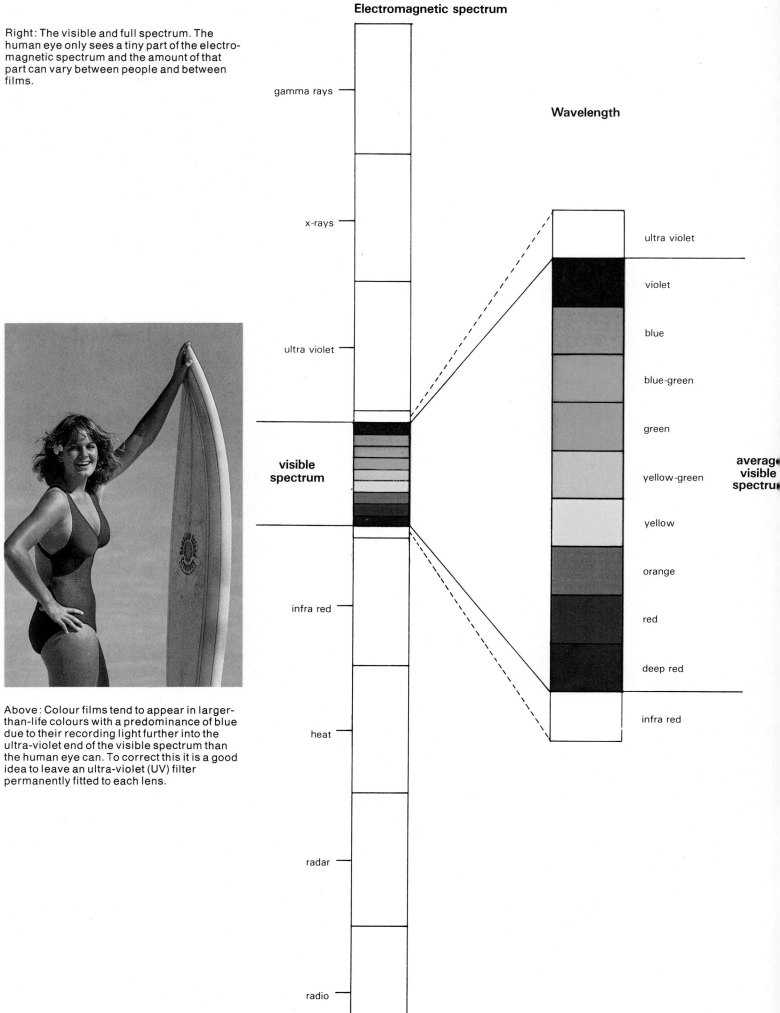

Right: The visible and full spectrum. The
human eye only sees a tiny part of the electromagnetic spectrum and the amount of that
part can vary between people and between
films.

Electromagnetic spectrum

Wavelength

gamma rays

x-rays

ultra violet

**visible
spectrum**

infra red

heat

radar

radio

ultra violet

violet

blue

blue-green

green

yellow-green

yellow

orange

red

deep red

infra red

**averag
visible
spectru**

Above: Colour films tend to appear in larger-
than-life colours with a predominance of blue
due to their recording light further into the
ultra-violet end of the visible spectrum than
the human eye can. To correct this it is a good
idea to leave an ultra-violet (UV) filter
permanently fitted to each lens.

Peterborough market square photographed by streetlight on daylight colour-corrected film. A correction filter would have removed the warm tone and spoiled the picture.

The reason for the need to make corrections when the light source changes is a simple one, yet it causes many arguments whenever photographers compare notes, for contrary to popular opinion our films judge colours more accurately than we do. Light itself is but a small part of the electromagnetic spectrum, measured in angstrom units and extending from gamma rays through to X-rays and on to infra-red, followed by heat, radar and so on to wireless waves. Of this spectrum only a tiny part, from the edges of ultra-violet to just beyond deep red, is visible to the human eye, yet our film can see more.

Human eyes are not uniform; some will be biased to one end or even one part of the spectrum scale. But while our vision can be sufficiently biased to verge on colour blindness, we all too easily tend to criticize the colour of our film. Photographers will argue about which type or make of colour film gives a better result, when frankly the choice is ours. The film's colours are in the eye of the beholder, and we also have to allow for the fact that its visible spectrum is greater.

World water ski
champion Mike
Hazlewood and the
ski scene below were
both subjects where
a UV filter was
essential. Water and
snow both reflect
back ultra-violet light
mirrored from the
sky and invisible to
us but all too visible
to film. This is why
our seaside pictures
always seem to
depict a deep blue
sea even though we
remember it as green
or even muddy
brown. The higher
the altitude the
clearer the air and
therefore the greater
the ultra-violet
reflections.

Right: A beautiful
picture taken in un-
polluted tropical
light.

Right: Midday
Californian sunlight,
by which all other
light is judged.

Colour films can see colours further along the spectrum, especially into the ultra-violet range, that are completely invisible to the human eye, and these rays of light will appear as previously unseen tints in our final pictures. Blue skies become bluer, snow scenes, shadows, oceans and lakes – all of which reflect ultra-violet back up to the sky – tend to appear bluer in our colour pictures than we remember or wished for. Fortunately, though, this 'exaggeration' can be cured by the use of an ultra-violet filter.

Recognizing these problems in the early days of colour photography, and wanting to arrive at a standard, the advanced photographic countries met and decided that our films' spectrum should be set to relate as near as possible to the colour temperature of perfect noonday sun, and opted for a figure of 5,400° Kelvin (a smaller measuring unit of the angstrom). The nearest light to the perfect colour temperature was found to be in Southern California, and this led directly to the birth of Hollywood, in an area that had previously been a desert. From that daylight standard all other temperatures are measured, from the humble candle which gives 1,930°K to perfect blue sky at 18,000°K; household tungsten light is much redder at 2,400°K, and to correct between these colour temperatures we use colour-correction filters.

Since there is no such thing as an all-round film, the wise photographer carries several different types and is prepared to change film in mid-shoot if the need arises. Better still, he or she would use two different cameras, each loaded with different types of film, possibly one black-and-white, the other colour, to be used near-simultaneously.

Light and Exposure

Even the owner of an automatic camera will soon encounter situations where, for successful results, he or she must understand not just how the ambient or available light is affecting the subject, but also how the camera's meter and film will react. There are many times when an automatic-exposure system must be overridden, and this requires considerable understanding from the camera operator; more advanced photographers find they need to add a separate hand-held exposure meter to their range.

The beginner with a simple camera will know or remember the well-meant advice offered in both film and camera instructions, namely to keep the sun or the light source behind his or her right-hand shoulder. The purpose of this advice, however, is to *guarantee* a result. By drastically over-simplifying matters, this kind of instruction aims to make sure that the beginner avoids all problem areas which would be too complicated to explain in basic terms. But if the beginner is deliberately under-informed, he or she will never see their potential for taking better pictures.

Most rules are made to be broken, and in photography there is no better example of a breakable rule than the one which says you must keep the light source behind you. At a stroke it robs pictures of the essential shadows that can add such a considerable dimension. Shadows give form, shape and depth, and when coupled to the clever use of perspective these can make the simplest pictures jump off the page – a vivid slice of reality preserved in time.

An automatic or direct exposure reading would see this as merely a dark scene and suggest an exposure to lighten the subject, thereby overexposing. An invercone reading is preferable.

Don't always keep the sun behind you for it is only the back lighting that has given the soft fluffy texture to this brood of ducks.

Harsh side lighting has lifted out this beautiful picture of Bjorn Borg, whilst the telephoto's lack of depth has successfully killed off the background.

If you walk right around your subject at noon on a bright, sunny day, just observing the light changes and without a camera, you will see that by moving approximately 45° from a starting position with the sun behind you, the colours and textures become far more interesting.

The portrait photographer, for instance, would begin to see texture in skin, cloth and hair that was previously invisible, while colours would become more saturated and defined until eventually, having reached 180° and moved into back lighting, there would be almost a halo-rim light effect. This in effect is no more than the studio photographer does every day by moving his portable sun or lights about, yet those studio lights cannot begin to compare with nature and the power of the sun, coupled with the immense reflecting capacity of the sky.

If you repeat the experiment early or late in the day, this time with the sun low in the sky, then naturally each of those earlier observed effects would be greatly exaggerated, possibly too much so for some subjects. The portrait, for example, could become unflatteringly harsh.

Meanwhile the exposure meter, whether built-in or a separate hand-held instrument, is flummoxed, because it is set to read an average subject and we have just changed the rules. It would be equally flummoxed by any dark

Struggling for sufficient light for this indoor basketball picture, the photographer waited until all of the players were looking upwards at the basket and of course their faces were then well illuminated by the prevailing top light.

The photographer here thought he was photographing his brother but in practice the strong back light from the windows has fooled his automatic-exposure camera. An invercone reading back to the camera from the subject would not have been influenced by those windows at all.

or light colour predominating in the subject. This merely illustrates that the meter can't think for us, and that it must be used with common sense. The lessons are: only read the light that is actually falling on the subject itself, not its background, and only read it from the camera's taking direction.

Left to its own devices, the meter cannot cope with subjects such as an expanse of snow, sky or water, or areas of dark shadow, for these cannot be averaged. All meters are calibrated to a standard grey card, on the basis that they will only be asked to read light reflected from a range of average subjects, a mixture of dark and light tones that if mixed together would average out to a single grey tone.

Imagine a good sunny day in which the subject is a figure set in a landscape and viewed from a distance. So long as all the tones are represented in fairly equal proportions, the meter can cope. Should you, however, lower your own viewpoint so as to take that same picture against the sky, which would then be predominant, the meter would alter its reading to a non-existent average and be hopelessly wrong; the end-result would be under-exposure. In such circumstances, what you have to do is take your exposure readings with the camera or meter tilted downwards, i.e. so that it records the average scene. The answer will then be true for the figure, which has not moved – only the camera moved – and is still receiving the same amount of light.

Continuing this theme, suppose that same figure within that same general scene happened to be wearing either a black or white dress, and that we now wish to move to close-up, to photograph the figure alone. What then?

In the previous photographs the dress was too small within the total scene to make any significant exposure difference. Now it is the predominant area seen in close-up; and although, as before, the light level is identical, once again the meter will fail, hopelessly confused by the colours.

In this side-to-backlit shot the author failed to recognize just how much light the hat of American triple world motorcycle racing champion Kenny Roberts was holding off his face. The moral is to remove the hat or change the angle of the camera or the subject.

43

Automation or direct exposure reading would have turned this into-the-sun picture into a silhouette. Only the invercone (below) can really cope. Using this, the exposure meter only reads light falling onto the subject from the camera's position. Ideally the reading should be taken from the subject to the camera but as in most cases the same light is falling on the camera as on the subject it will usually be adequate to point the invercone rearward from the camera position.

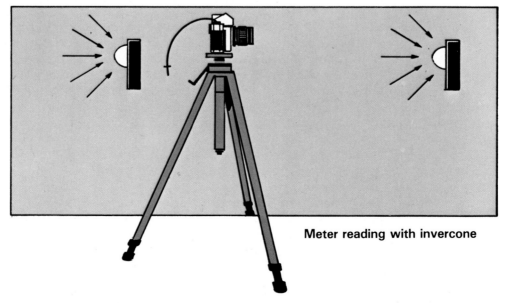

Meter reading with invercone

A white dress – it's the same for a snowy background – would fool our meter into deciding that the light was brighter than before. This is because white reflects back more light than grey (the average), and so the suggested exposure image would be underexposed. Conversely a black dress would suggest darkness, and the meter would propose a setting that would pass more light to the film, so lightening the average back to grey; the result would be overexposure.

When you begin to use side or back lighting, especially when the light source or sun is low, even actually in the picture, then you must only read the light actually falling onto the part of the subject to be seen by the camera. The hardest part is learning to recognize the symptoms in the first place; once recognized, the cure is simple, and like most photographic problems is only a matter of common sense.

When in doubt, try taking your readings from an average subject nearby. It can be a different subject from the eventual one, but should be receiving the same amount of light. As a double check, turn through 180° and read the light from the opposite direction with the sun now behind you. As a rough guide, your second reading should be appreciably brighter than the first; if not, your intended picture will be underexposed and in silhouette.

By far the safest way is to use a separate exposure meter with an invercone attachment. This is operated by pointing the meter in an exactly opposite direction to the camera, and so cuts out confusing extraneous light. The invercone is like half a ping pong ball placed over the measuring cell, and its job is to collect the direct and stray light reaching the subject, and to average it out.

At first glance both the above are difficult exposures, but in each case the water or snow actually acts like a giant reflector, sending light back into these shadow areas on backlit subjects and so easing the exposure interpretation with an invercone.

The difference between this and other types of meter is that by pointing it in the opposite direction to the camera, it becomes like the subject, i.e. it cannot see or be confused by light behind it – light which, although looking bright in the viewfinder, does not increase the illumination of the subject.

Once this lesson has been absorbed, you are in a position to experiment or cheat, and manufacture pictures by deliberately under- or overexposing; by this means, for instance, you can turn night scenes into day, or vice versa. You can take apparent sunsets at mid-day simply by deliberately underexposing the picture when looking into and including the sun; you can also augment the deception on a colour film by adding an orange filter. You can make day scenes appear like night by shooting into the light while deliberately underexposing by approximately two stops, and by high-lighting or rimlighting those parts of the pictures that you need still to be able to recognize.

Watch out the next time there is a supposed night scene on film or TV. Sooner or later there will be a give-away: sun-fringed clouds, glinting car

Right: This hang-gliding picture could well have been taken by automatic exposure, as the sky's residual brilliance has suggested, and resulted in slight underexposure. However in this case this darkening has also brought about a pleasing deeper colour saturation and therefore works well.

Below: For those automatic-exposure cameras without manual override all is not lost. The top dials show the normal override method: when moved to the figure 2 twice as much light is passed. The lower dials do not appear to have this facility, but in practice all that is necessary is to temporarily adjust the film ASA setting from 200 ASA to 100 ASA to achieve the same end.

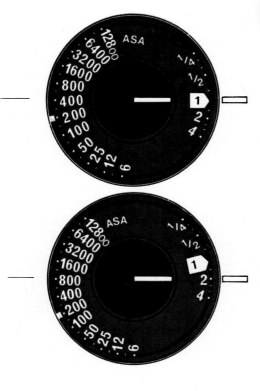

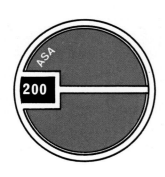

windows and the like are the clues to look for. But although the TV effect is deliberate, and is shot in daylight with the camera pointing into the sun, it is the same as a fully automatic non-manual-override camera would force upon us under such lighting conditions whether we liked it or not.

Many cameras without a manual switch-over facility are at least designed to recognize our eventual need to control, and as a compromise provide partial override; but even if they do not, all is not yet lost. Partial overrides usually take the form of a plus or minus control knob linked to either the shutter or aperture settings to increase or decrease the amount of light passed by up to 2 stops.

Once you know when automation will be beaten, you can correct its mistakes by pointing the camera down to check what the exposure should be, and then up to check what the exposure would be if automation was left to its own devices. If the downward exposure is appreciably more or less, then the override control must be moved in a plus or minus direction until the indicated exposure reading, when looking at the final framing, is the same as the one received when looking downwards. If you have no override correction, you can still find a way around this problem. Use exactly the same exposure-reading techniques, but then alter the camera meter's film-speed setting ring accordingly. Frankly, neither of these alternatives is ideal, primarily because it is then all too easy to forget that the settings have been altered, and then move on to another subject which does not need alteration. For this reason, though all my own cameras have each type of automatic facility inbuilt, I still take 90% of my pictures with the camera set manually, and only use the camera's meter as a guide.

There can be situations, of course, where an average subject cannot be found for a reading; without an invercone meter, they may seem to pose insoluble problems. Vast snowscapes or sea scenes fall into this category; but do not be put off, there are a couple of simple ways of achieving success which, though not entirely accurate, are at least as good as an educated guess and worth trying.

Firstly, when faced with this kind of problem, remember that human flesh is a lot nearer in tone to grey than ever your background will be. So move in and take the reading through the camera, filling the image with a face or even your own hand. Secondly, if telephoto lenses are available, it may well be possible to pull up a more average area of the distant scene, for example the treeline in a snowscape. In either instance your exposure should be within one half a stop of accuracy; so to play safe, bracket the exposures. In other words, if your educated guess suggests 1/250 sec. at f5.6, then after taking a picture at that setting take two more frames, one on either side, i.e. 1/250 sec. at f4.5 and 1/250 at f6.3. Before anyone suggests that such settings are not mentioned on their lenses, they are in fact midway between the fully calibrated stops; thus f4.5 falls between f4 and f5.6.

Left and below: These evening scenes have been captured perfectly by means of time exposure. In such instances one should allow approximately two stops less than the meter suggested.

Meter reading

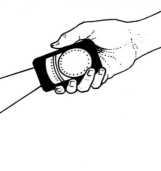

Left: When an invercone meter is not available, simply point the camera or meter downwards to cut out most of the sky from the reading.

The Great Outdoors

Although firm photographic foundations need an understanding of basic theory, it is also true that only with practice will your photographs get better. This book can help to cut some corners in the quest for good pictures, but it is only when you are out taking pictures that you experience the real thrill of photography.

Sometimes, though, people remain stuck because they can't think of anything to photograph. Although they now have the motivation, and the basic theory behind them, they do not have the experience to look at their own backyard and see it as a storehouse of scenes.

Ironically, when the summer holidays come round, vast numbers of camera-armed citizens plan journeys crossing their own country, even the world, to photograph the other side. Meanwhile, people whose homelands they were about to invade are busy planning photo trips in the opposite direction! How interesting and enlightening it would be for each to look at the others' results, to see their own daily environment proudly captured through the eyes of others. What would people make of all those shots of scenes which in the past they had ignored, walking right past them.

One way round this problem of finding a starting point is to set yourself a series of challenges, or exercises. Plan them to extend both yourself and the camera, and never mind what the weather may bring. Begin with a set theme and aim to complete them as a weekly or even daily exercise. For example, the city-dweller might consider beginning with lists of subjects along the following lines:

1 *Age and antiquity*. This could cover people or places or even just a piece of old or new timber.
2 *Grime*. Look for subjects ranging from garbage tossed in the street to graffiti on walls or vehicles.
3 *Rush Hour*. Show people jostling and rushing in the streets and subways, traffic jams, etc.
4 *Beauty on the Street*. Probably animal, but could be anything you fancy.

Photographed back-lit, this weather-beaten disused railway line in Arizona makes a simple yet pleasing picture.

Back lighting has given added interest to this snapshot of a San Francisco street.

An easy picture of Rye, a quiet back-water in rural England. The photographer has waited for a time of day when there is just enough soft shadow on the street to provide some contrasting light and has used passing figures to add interest to the scene.

5 *Rain*. People sheltering, patterns of umbrellas and reflections in puddles.

6 *Shopping*. From the wonderment of children to the cautious elderly, in streets, shops and markets.

7 *The Park*. Most cities have inner parks which provide a peaceful lunchtime oasis where people rest, read, cuddle, and feed themselves and the birds.

8 *The Washing*. Gaily coloured washing can often be seen lightening drab tenements, translucent against the sky, or flapping in the breeze. Alternatively, the theme might suggest washing a car or building.

9 *Dusk to Dawn*. Could be an entire feature on a day in the life of a city, with sunrises and sunsets glinting off tower block windows.

10 *Leaves*. From tree-lined avenues to rotting bark or fallen leaves.

11 *Faces*. Look for expressions – of joy, anger, boredom, frustration – in massed gatherings or isolated on one face in a crowd.

12 *Light and Shade*. High shadows and towering buildings, where sunlight hardly reaches ground level, can make for fascinating black-and-white or colour patterns.

Above and top left: Simple but pleasing scenes with movement taken while enjoying a family holiday at the beach.

Top right: A contrived sunset. This picture was actually taken at midday and deliberately underexposed.

Facing page: A most difficult moving picture as it is always harder to judge movement away from the camera. It was taken during the author's coverage of the Lake Placid Winter Olympics in the U.S.A.

Twelve examples of simple subjects: each on its own would make a full photographic feature, yet these are the kinds of subject that are so easily passed by. The country-dweller can compile a similar list of what are really obvious themes, and each could then expand the list to include topics such as the four seasons or even the times of day. It requires only a little imagination to see that the possibilities are almost endless.

Given this kind of challenge, not only do you learn photographic awareness, you are using your camera all the time no matter what the weather on an infinitely varying range of subjects. Your pictures are bound to improve.

CAPTURING MOVEMENT

If you choose sport or an action theme, you will need to know a little more. But provided the lessons of the earlier chapters have been learned, any such subjects can be tackled with success.

Rapidly moving subjects need more than just a high shutter speed to freeze the action. You need to learn to pan, and also to decide how much apparent or background movement you require.

Imagine a racing car travelling at 120 miles per hour; it actually covers 54 metres (176 feet) a second. Even if you set your shutter speed at 1/1000 sec. and take the picture without moving the camera, the car during the exposure time would have travelled several feet and hopelessly blur the image. If, on the other hand, you pan the camera, i.e. move the camera with the car, then in practice car and camera no longer move in relationship to each other. It is now the background which is rushing by at 120 miles per hour. A high shutter speed ceases to be important, even 1/15 sec. would suffice; so long as the pan is accurate, the simplest box camera could cope with this subject – and would incidentally provide a beautifully blurred backdrop to give a real impression of speed.

Panning is worth practising by any stretch of fast road – and you don't need film in the camera to master the technique. Stand with your feet wide apart and your shoulders square to the road, tucking in both elbows and holding the camera firmly and well into the chest. The upper and lower halves of your body should be as rigid as possible, but you remain free to pivot from the waist and hips.

This stance is not unlike that of the golfer, and almost the same principles are involved, because the next move is to pivot from the waist in the direction of the approaching car and pick it up in your viewfinder. You then follow through, pivoting with the car as it passes and disappears. At the mid-point of the pan the car should be absolutely central in the viewfinder, and your shoulders square to the road. This is the moment to take the picture – but don't forget to follow through.

If your movement was fluid and accurate, then at no time would you have needed to speed up or slow down to maintain the car's image in the centre of the viewfinder. Had you taken a picture, it would have been sharp even at the slowest shutter speed, with an impressive background blur. If you have to speed up or slow down during the pan then the pan is not accurate and the picture will fail.

This panning principle applies equally to slower-moving subjects like children, athletes, dogs and horses, but while the car's movement is in one direction only, humans and animals have arms and legs that flail about in all directions. And although they appear to be slower, those limbs will need a much higher speed to freeze them (such as 1/500 sec.) even though you pan in time with the main body movement. However, blurred arms, legs and backgrounds can give excellent impressions of speed and movement, so experiment and don't over-freeze, or else the picture may turn out sharp all over but disappointing as a portrayal of movement.

Kodak once had an advertising campaign that used the theme 'Carry a Camera'. Their object at the time was to sell film, but the slogan is a good one and even better if it is enlarged to 'Carry a Camera at the Ready'.

We tend to purchase cameras complete with so-called ever-ready cases (ERC), and then add accessories and film, and then we need something larger to carry the whole outfit in, and in doing so often become less mobile, unable to act spontaneously. To be physically ready to take pictures requires quite some thought, for we have to balance mobility and speed with adequate protection for equipment which may well be our most valuable, as well as our proudest, possession.

The camera's purpose is to take pictures, not to be a wrapped in some cotton-wool showpiece; naturally it needs looking after and regular cleaning and checks, but it should also be kept, carried, and even stored in a state of maximum readiness. Ever-ready camera cases, lens or meter cases and film cartons may at first glance appear to be perfect protective devices, but each will delay, maybe even deter, their owner from actually taking pictures.

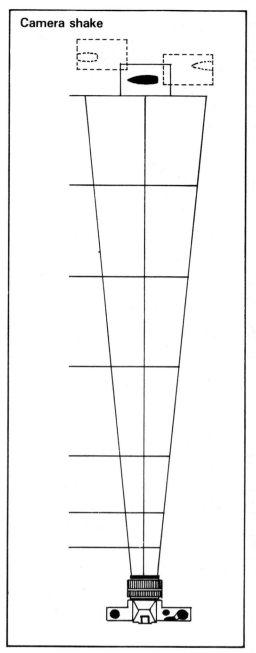

Camera shake

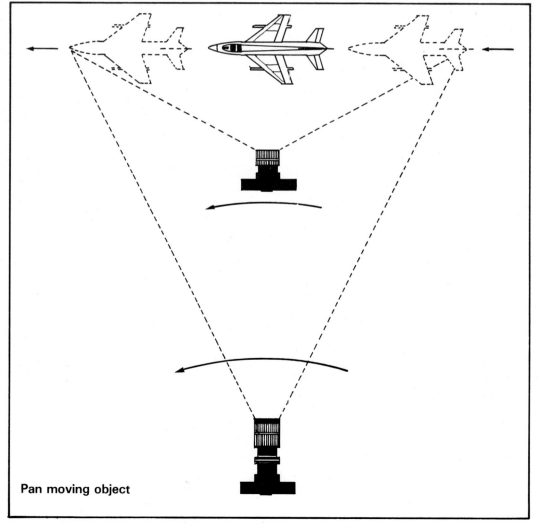

Pan moving object

Above: The effect of camera shake is to give the subject the appearance of movement, and is emphasized with longer lenses leading to blurred pictures. It is essential therefore to develop a good picture-taking stance with the arms tucked well into the chest to form a human tripod.

Left: Panning with rapid movement is easier from a distance when the subject's motion is easier to follow. Pick up the aircraft early, as in this case, and follow its progress right through in the viewfinder. Take the picture only if the aircraft has stayed central throughout the pan: if the photographer has to speed up or slow down his action, then the aircraft and the camera will be moving at different speeds in relationship to each other and the picture will blur.

Motor drives or power winders are ideal for recording sequences such as this where pictures are required in rapid succession.

Try and devise something faster. Ideally the camera should be ready loaded, and unfettered even by an ever-ready case – which will eventually need removing if only to re-load with fresh film. Discard such impediments, and prepare an additional, uncartoned supply of film; this should be packed, like other lenses or accessories, immediately to hand.

Thought on these lines will be amply repaid by the numbers of instant pictures you take *and* in the hard cash you save by not buying pretty but useless carrying cases.

The best type of camera bag is the all-purpose traveller's shoulder bag, preferably fitted with plenty of separate pockets and partitions, many of which could very well have been designed with photographers in mind, but which are invariably cheaper than their specialist photographic counterparts. Cheap, and available in all sizes, these bags perfectly accommodate the camera equipment along with anything else you might wish to carry. What's more, they can be used from the shoulder and while on the move.

It pays to devise and memorize a bag-loading system, so that without even looking you know precisely what is in each pocket. For instance, put long lenses in the front compartment, wide-angles in the rear, black-and-white film left, colour right, and so on. To keep cameras and lenses from rubbing against each other, use something like well-washed household dusters to wrap them in. These can be quickly removed without fumbling and take up little space in the bag.

Films in makers' cartons take up an enormous amount of space and need a considerable time to unwrap. To simplify that job, before you set out for the day's assignment, re-load the unwrapped films four at a time into small plastic containers; the type used for returning processed transparencies will do very well. As an added safeguard, write which type of film is enclosed on the container, and to streamline the operation further, make a habit of standing all unused cassettes one way up, and replacing the used ones upside-down or the opposite way round. Systems like this increase your carrying capacity, reduce the risk of re-loading used film, and allow spot-checks at any time – this is especially useful where several film packs or containers are involved.

With a zip bag loaded and on the shoulder, you can be ready to shoot almost instantly, and you can choose and assemble your equipment by feel, without the need to stop and put the bag down. Finally, on the subject of carrying bags, choose a size with a little more room than you need for your photographic equipment. Then you can also use it for useful items like maps, waterproofs, sunglasses . . . and lunch.

Many camera manufacturers market sumptuous-looking attaché case holdalls or outfit cases, which look great but tend to be unpractical, and with the manufacturer's name on them are an advertisement to thieves.

FILTERS

Earlier, we looked at the advantages of using an ultra-violet or skylight filter, both to do the job for which it was designed, and also to protect valuable lenses from rain and dust. The simplest, cheapest and best systems follow the COKIN principle. Instead of the usual round screw-in filters, to which the camera lens is added, a square, combined filter-holder and lens-hood is fixed more or less permanently to each lens; the matching standard-size square filters fit into the assembly like a drawer into the hood itself.

This is a brilliant idea, since square-format hoods are far better for keeping stray light and rain away from the lens. Coupled with cheaper and universal-size filters, you then need only one example of each type or colour for complete interchangeability in your lens range. It is also simple to use polarizing filters, which need to be rotated for maximum effect, or graduated filters which filter just one part of the scene; these can easily be moved within the lens-hood filter slot.

This camera outfit case looks beautiful but is unpractical and expensive. It is better to use a soft flexible airline-type shoulder bag.

BLACK-AND-WHITE WORK

Most problems to do with filtration, whether in black-and-white or colour, arise because the sun and sky are so much brighter than the rest of the view, and will inevitably burn out on negatives.

A common complaint in black-and-white photography is that those well-remembered puffy white clouds have disappeared from the finished print. The practical cause of this loss is partly due to the similarity of grey and light-blue tones when both are produced as greys in black-and-white, and partly because the sky, being so much brighter than the rest of the subject, tends to overexpose to total black on the negative. To cure those problems and restore your clouds, you need either to reduce the overall sky exposure, or to place a coloured filter over the lens which will hold back the predominant blue sky colour.

In either solution you need a filter with a colour at the opposite end of the visible spectrum to blue, i.e. anywhere between yellow and red, so that it will pass the grey or white image of the cloud formation unaltered, but hold back the overall sky blue. A mild yellow filter such as a 2 × will produce a mild cloud image; alternatively a strong red 6 or 7 × will give an exaggerated impression, suggesting that a storm was brewing on what was really a beautiful summer day.

54

Professionals tend to use photo vests with many storage pockets rather than an outfit case so as to free arms and shoulders for rapid movement and instant availability of equipment. The author, so equipped, is here chatting to Kenny Roberts at Laguna Seca Raceway, California.

If you are to filter at all, then you might just as well exaggerate the effect, so rather than carry a whole range of filters you could make do with just one. A definite orange, such as 4 or 5 ×, would exaggerate nicely, yet not take too much light away from the film – for that factor of 4 or 5 × refers to the amount of light the filter is holding back, not just from the sky but also from the rest of the subject, and which needs to be compensated for in those other areas. To make up for that lost light, you need to open up the aperture or slow down the shutter speed by that factor. This is in fact rather a lot of light and can't always be spared, especially on slow film. A further disadvantage of the all-over filter is that not only does it filter the sky, it also changes the overall tone balance, possibly to the detriment of the rest of the scene which did not need filtration.

Graduated filters can solve this problem. They change gradually in tone and colour, beginning as clear glass, and can be moved in the filter slot to filter just that area of the picture that needs attention, leaving the rest. By moving the filter up or down the lens-hood while looking through an SLR camera, you can actually inspect the effect and fix a cut-off point so that you only filter those areas that need it; on a non-reflex camera, you have to do this by guesswork. Now you have reduced the overpowering sky illumination without having to increase the overall exposure, and you have done this without altering the colour balance or tones on the main subject.

COLOUR WORK

As colour reversal films are balanced specifically for daylight or photoflood lamps, any other light source which will have a different temperature on the spectrum scale will alter the film's final image colours. This effect is known as a colour cast. There are available a range of correction filters to balance those imperfect light sources, such as fluorescent light which is much greener than daylight or tungsten and would make any unfiltered pictures appear green.

Without filtration, candlelight or street neons would appear warmer or redder, whilst anything illuminated by an arc light would appear bluer, and so on. However, we can ignore most of these other casts, for in many ways they can help the picture. After all, no-one would want to correct that intimate warm candlelight to look like daylight!

For colour work outdoors in sunshine, we do need an ultra-violet or skylight protection filter, otherwise UV light, unseen by human eyes, will record as an overall blue or cold tone that could well spoil the finished picture. As with black-and-white shots, colour photographers may also wish to darken the sky, or lift out some cloud. Again, you would use a graduated filter, but because you can't afford to change the colour scheme, you would choose a filter of the same colour, e.g. blue graduated.

All rules can be broken, though, and by using other filter colours out of context on colour film you can cheat with success. For instance, you could add an orange filter of the kind intended only for black-and-white photography, and shoot into the sun with it to exaggerate or even manufacture a sunset.

An all-over colour filter would naturally affect the whole scene, changing all the colours to an overall cast in its own colour. It is better to use the graduated filter as before, to change just that part of the scene that needs it. There are additional filters for use with either black-and-white or colour films, such as the polarizing and starburst type, each of which can be worth owning and carrying since they can help to dramatize an otherwise lacklustre subject.

The polarizing filter has almost a double role; it acts in the same way as sunglasses on human eyes, cutting out that glare which could so easily desaturate the essential colours. Its main purpose is to remove or at least reduce annoying reflections off surfaces like windows or water, allowing the lens to see through to the other side, as, for example, with a shop window. The polarizing filter is in fact two filters sandwiched together, each of which only passes light in one wavelength. By rotating one filter against the other while looking through an SLR, we can see the point at which the two filters cut out the unwanted wavelengths or reflections. Unfortunately this setting needs to be changed with each viewpoint, and whenever the camera is turned from the vertical to the horizontal; another disadvantage is that the dark grey in colour filters loses almost a quarter of the light which would have otherwise reached the film.

To brighten up the winter scene a grey graduated Cokin filter was used to darken the sky and a polarizing filter to remove water reflection and exaggerate colour.

A natural winter waterscape taken without a filter.

Here the photographer has contrived a sunset effect by using an orange filter to alter an otherwise lacklustre subject.

The starburst is simply a colourless glass onto which are engraved a series of fine criss-cross lines. These lines do not record on the picture themselves, but when pointed into the light source they cause internal reflections which appear on the film like tiny stars. These filters work particularly well on backlit and water scenes, where the sunlit ripples of water transform into myriads of tiny glistening stars, but they only work provided there are such points of light in the picture. For starbursts, no exposure compensation is required.

At the end of a day's shooting, check and clean the cameras and lenses with a clean, if old, linen handkerchief. Avoid solvents or tissues such as spectacle cleaners, which can harm the coating of a camera lens. If the camera has got wet, even in prolonged rain, it won't come to any harm so long as it is dried off properly and as soon as possible with a towel and finished with the handkerchief. Do not put it on a radiator to dry because this makes for internal condensation. Try to avoid moving the camera directly from cold outdoor conditions to a hot room, as the resultant internal condensation could cause far more harm than any moisture on the outside of the camera. Finally, remember to switch off the exposure-meter system if it is battery-powered.

Not a filter but a multi-image prism which simply screws into the front of the lens and can then be rotated until the desired effect is achieved.

Photography in Poor Light

Working in poor light stretches not just the photographer's skills, but the potential subject range too. This can be divided roughly into two categories: subjects that can and should be tackled with whatever light is available, no matter how dim, and those that need additional lights such as flash or studio photoflood.

Here more than ever you need to understand the workings of the camera, lenses, film, and light itself because now you will be forced to cut back on the safety margins as you go for your pictures. The first thing to remember is that if you have a fast lens and film, then you can photograph anything that the eye can see. You can do so either by treating your subjects naturally, by using the light available, or you can deliberately add extra but unnatural light sources.

As a starting point, let us consider those subjects over which we have little or no control – an indoor or floodlit outdoor sports meeting, for example, where flash or photoflood lighting would be banned for fear of affecting or momentarily blinding the participants. The obvious first step is to establish how much light is actually available. This will determine the speed of film and the lens combination. To help you assess low light conditions, it is best to have an invercone type of meter (as described on page 45). If possible, take your reading from the playing area, reading back to the

Olympic champion Shaposhnicova whilst winning a gold medal in Moscow. The white leotard reflected almost a whole stop more light into the gymnast's face than a darker coloured leotard would have, which required raising the shutter speed from 1/125 sec. to 1/250 sec.

Where the ambient light level is just too low to allow a high enough shutter speed to freeze movement, then why not deliberately blur? The author contrived the picture by exposing for $\frac{1}{4}$ sec. into backlight.

A variation of the theme is the zoom burst, achieved by concertinaing a zoom lens's focal-length shift barrel during a slow $\frac{1}{4}$-sec. exposure.

intended camera position. The reason for this is that most large sports arenas are lit by floodlights positioned above and behind the perimeter and set to converge; they tend therefore to be unevenly lit. Tennis, squash, gymnastics, table tennis, football and baseball pitches, netball, basketball, show jumping, speedway and boxing all have top lighting which more often than not is uneven; usually it is brightest in such areas as the goal and dimmest in the centre of the court or pitch.

The best way is to arrive early and ask if either you or an official can take your exposure meter out on to the arena so that you can read back. Try to take these exposure readings from all round, or at least at each end and in the middle of the pitch or court, and then stick to those readings for the entire event no matter what the camera's meter might tell you.

Should it prove impossible to take on-court readings, then once again you must fall back on an intuitive estimate based on experience; if so, try to read through a long lens off an average tone, such as grass, which is receiving the same amount of light as the players. Remember that if this available light is very low in intensity, it will help if you move higher up the stadium. The predominant top light will then be travelling in approximately the same direction as the camera angle, and will be slightly brighter.

When you take your reading, relate the light value indicated by the exposure meter to that of the film speed and read off. The result might well be a maximum shutter-speed/aperture combination of 1/250 sec. at f2.8. Slower shutter speeds would not stop subject movement, but don't overlook the deliberately blurred shots which can be just as pleasing. These can be achieved by choosing a setting such as 1/15 sec. at f11; ideally, use a tripod or monopod (single-leg support) to reduce camera shake. Great blur effects can be achieved by deliberately panning in the opposite direction to the moving subject, or by altering the zoom lens's optical length, working it like a trombone during the exposure process. For the best effect you really want some part of the action to be at least recognizable, if not sharp, a player's body for instance, while everything else – arms, legs, ball, etc. – is vividly blurred.

For the most part, of course, you want pictures that are sharp, and this brings us back to the likely setting of 1/250 sec. at f2.8, and two basic problems that need to be overcome. Firstly, a 1/250 sec. setting is not really enough to stop movements that you can't pan with, as when players converge on each other from opposite directions. Secondly, with longer lenses you have virtually no depth of field.

When movement is both sudden and dramatic, such as the boxer's punch or the basketball player's leap for the net, there is a good possibility that your maximum shutter speed will still be insufficient to freeze the action. The

Aim for the moment of inertia when in real terms the motion has stopped. These basketball players have reached the peak of action and are on the point of reversing.

Steaming Joe Frazier taking a break in training and allowing the author to expose at 1/30 at f2.

solution lies in the nature of movement. All movement stops somewhere – this point is known as the point of inertia. Simple examples are when the punch has landed or the basketball player has reached the highest point of his or her leap. For minute fractions of time, movement actually stops, and so you no longer need a high shutter speed to isolate it. The object is thus to take your picture at that exact moment, when the scene will appear successfully frozen and sharp.

To achieve this aim requires some skill, particularly when you are using an SLR camera with its internal-mirror delay. The trick is to anticipate the peak moment, telling the finger to press the shutter *before* the peak is reached. Practise this with games like tennis or table tennis. As an initial exercise, set yourself the task of getting the ball in picture on a tight close-up shot of only one player. This is very difficult to achieve, yet without the ball in the picture the shot will lack purpose and be a failure.

The second problem, the lack of depth of field, also deserves some thought and practice. Here again the need to anticipate is important if you are to capture a subject who has moved beyond the point on which you had pre-focused. Two possible solutions are either to focus on an imaginary point just in front of the athlete, in the area that he or she is about to move into, or to predetermine the eventual spot that he or she is aiming for. An example of the latter is the footballer or basketball player running for the net or goal. You could permanently focus on that area alone, ignoring the rest of the field of play, and wait for the action to come to you.

Tennis and table tennis can be similarly treated by opting only for baseline or net pictures, while the gymnast on the beam, rings or bars stays in an easily pre-definable area. With show jumping, which is easiest of all, you can just focus on the jump top.

Sports action is an extreme category, but its many inherent problems offer a varied challenge and a continual source of pictures needing to be taken in poor light. The experience you can gain from taking sports pictures can equally be applied to much more static and simple subjects, in the home and outdoors, which call for natural lighting, though low in level. This can be so much more pleasing and effective than the harshness of flash.

Indoor portraiture can benefit greatly from using available light only. A single window can provide the sole light source, with the sitter positioned next to the window and set preferably against a plain wall; this will give a marvellously natural modelling light. You can also use changes in the quality of light to bring out the best in particular subjects.

On a dull day the light is softer indoors, and more even, whereas a bright sunlit day will give a harsh light with deep shadow. Shadowy areas can always be softened or lightened by placing a piece of plain white card or paper out of picture and opposite the light source to reflect light back into the shadows.

Natural light is in any event better than artificial, and the above examples merely demonstrate principles that have been applied in painters' studios for centuries, and are used by fashion and portrait photographers today. Not everybody has a suitable room, however, or can guarantee that their photographic pursuits can all be fitted into the daylight hours, so the next and logical stage is to set up an artifically lit studio with light available at the turn of a switch.

A deliberate movement shot. Note how the athletes' legs and arms move like pistons but the heads and torsos stay basically sharp on this slow (1/15 sec.) panned shot.

USING FLASHLIGHTS

Home studios are perfectly practicable in the average, even small living room or bedroom, needing little other than a supply of power points for the lights or flash guns, and a choice of plain and coloured backdrops. There is

A simple home studio arrangement. The back light as drawn and shining through the paper could be moved to the side of the background roll. The purpose of the light is to light the paper not the model.

no need to paint the walls, for the backdrops can be bought as paper rolls from photographic shops or paper merchants and either strung up and hung from suitable hooks, or stood on home-made portable stands.

The choice of lights is between electronic flash or tungsten. Remember that what you are really trying to do is recreate the sun, and that wherever your lights are placed, and no matter how many are used, they should never conflict with each other. A good starting point would be to have one light and a white reflector, possibly a projector screen which you can use to simulate that earlier window setting in daylight. The main light should be at a position 45° above and to the side of the subject and the camera; this gives some shadow which in itself gives shape and form.

From this stage you probably need to experiment. Try replacing the reflector with a second but less powerful light to do the same job, and adding a third light to shine on and illuminate the backdrop only. A fourth light might be set behind the sitter but out of picture, shining back almost at the camera as a hair light, to shine through the subject's hair and give sparkle, texture, and so on. Do remember that no matter how many lights you add, they are only to supplement, never to overpower the main light which is your mobile sun. Now you are set to recreate any daylight scene.

Whether the studio lighting should be flash or tungsten is of little consequence to the expert, who understands lighting and merely chooses the correct colour-balanced daylight film if using flash, or tungsten for floodlights; but for the beginner tungsten lights are much simpler to use as their effects can be seen and studied.

A very simple alternative, or instant studio, might appear to be a single flashgun mounted on the camera's own accessory shoe, and indeed such devices are extremely useful as a last resort after dark outdoors, but should be avoided indoors if possible. There are two main problems with camera-mounted flashes. Firstly, as when the sun is behind you, flash lighting tends to be unduly flat; worse still, it will project harsh subject shadows onto walls or objects behind the subject.

Secondly, human eyes act as mirrors, so that when photographing people some of the light bounces straight back towards the camera, recording on the picture like car headlights, and turning mother-in-law into a fair impression of Dracula's mistress. This effect, when seen in colour, shows the sitter's eyes taking on the residual flash colour, and is known as 'red eye', a far from pretty or successful result.

The cure for both problems is either to get the flashgun away from the camera, either at arm's length, which is difficult if not impossible with most of today's small computer guns, or to use what is known as 'bounce flash'. To do this, point the flashgun either up to the ceiling or, if that is too high, behind you at the nearest wall, so that its light bounces all over the room; by the time it reaches the subject it is virtually non-directional and therefore shadowless. Unfortunately, much of the flash's power is lost this way as the light has to travel much further and much of it is soaked up by furniture and floors and never reaches the subject. This really means that a much more powerful flashgun is needed.

Most modern electronic flashguns have a small computer and a light sensor built-in, their job being to read how much light is bounced back from the subject to the gun, and then to set the exposure accordingly. When the flash's computer judges the subject to have received enough light, it merely switches or cuts off the flash duration; as a result, its exposure time can be infinitely variable between approximately 1/2000 sec. and 1/20000 sec.

You may wish to couple several portable flashguns together, virtually as a mobile studio, in which case you will have to use them manually. The reason is that the computers are built-in and therefore only act on light received back to their own position, rather than in the camera's direction. If you have two portable guns then, assuming that they can couple to the camera via a coaxial flash lead rather than exclusively via an accessory or hot shoe, you can place them in exactly the same way as you would position floodlights.

Below: Young Gary Morley rather badly photographed by the author using a flash. Note how flat the lighting is and the unpleasant shadow area projected by the flash onto the background caused by taking the photograph from this position.

Right: Ex-Miss World Julie Edge gets a helping hand in the author's home studio set-up. Normally those helpers would of course have been cut out of the finished picture.

64

Julie Edge again, taken on the same set-up as the previous picture but with a change of background paper colour.

Flash No. 1, set to deliver full power, takes the 45° main light position, and Flash No. 2, preferably set at half power in order not to conflict, is used on the opposite side as the fill-in light. They can be coupled either via a 'T'-piece synchronizing plug and flash leads, or by a remote slave unit, which is a cheap and tiny electronic gadget which fits on to the second unit by a suction pad, and itself has a plug fitting for the flashgun's lead. The slave unit is just an on-off switch operated by light and so its sensor should be pointed directly at the main gun. When that fires, the sensor switches on and works the fill-in flash remotely.

Because the flashguns have been set to the manual-exposure mode, you must then work out the flash or exposure factor from the instructions provided with the flashgun. Every gun has a flash-power factor quoted in figures, e.g. 100, set against a specific film speed. All you need to do is to divide the distance between the gun and the subject into the power-

Above: In this photograph two flashguns were used, both set up away from the camera on tripods and triggered by a slave unit. Each gun was placed fairly high and approximately 45° each side of the playing area.

factor figure, and the resulting figure is the correct aperture setting. For example, if the main gun is 10 ft from the subject, then 10 divided into 100 would give a correct aperture of f10. This is simple enough, but things get more complicated when a second gun is added to the equation.

Although two similarly powered and distance-set flashes would double the light, i.e. to f20, such a set-up really requires a proper and unfortunately expensive flash exposure meter to guarantee consistent results. A simple and much more economical compromise is to use one powerful computer gun set for automatic usage, though still at the 45° position, and to then add a very low-power second gun as a back light. The second gun can either rimlight the subject into camera, or illuminate just the backdrop or roll, but not the front of the subject as seen by the camera, and therefore does not alter the overall flash factor, which can then happily be left to the automatic computer.

Flash bulbs such as cube flashes are a cheap alternative without automation. The camera's aperture settings must be worked out for each picture via the film/bulb flash-factor chart supplied with the bulbs. Blue bulbs are for daylight colour film, and clear bulbs for artificial light.

Right: Multi-World Table Tennis Champion Stellan Bengtsson photographed using four separate and uncoupled flashguns and a time exposure. A different coloured gelatin filter was used over three of the guns to both reduce image exposure and change the colour, whilst the fourth and final gun produced the main correctly exposed and coloured image.

This picture of Paul Day won for the author the International Table Tennis Photographer Award, yet was taken under lighting that was almost impossibly low. By analyzing the action it was obvious that at the moment of serving there was just enough top light reflected back into the player's face from the white ball to make taking a picture possible.

When you are working with available light at the very lowest indoor-lighting extremes, shoot if in doubt straight up into the light. This will give you rimlit semi-silhouettes. Good examples are the basketball, tennis or table tennis players mentioned earlier. Even when the light level is so low that you cannot contemplate taking detailed action shots, you will at least end up with a picture – and there are many good picture studies to be had, almost action portraits, showing concentration and determination as the player, now quite still, waits to receive the ball. Because the player is static, you can then expose at appreciably lower shutter speeds.

If you also choose a very low angle, although much of the face will be in shade those parts nearest to or set against light will be dramatic, the drama perhaps boosted by reflections of glistening perspiration. Never mind that you are working at full aperture, that is what so much light-gathering power is for. It is far better to have the highest available shutter speed and to be sure of avoiding camera shake and unintentional subject blur; but do remember that your focusing must be precise.

NIGHT SCENES

One of the most fascinating and yet easiest areas of outdoor photography is the night scene – of streets, bonfires, fireworks, neon signs, and so on. Any type of film is suitable, so choose colour films by preference alone. A tripod is essential, though, to give the necessary long exposure time.

Exposure readings in these circumstances are so variable that you may as well ignore the exposure meter. The meter will still be aiming for an average grey tone, and therefore trying to transform your night scene into day. However, it is really very simple to work out the exposure by other means.

Take, for example, a street scene. There will usually be scores of distant but in fact very bright lights set amongst the seemingly pitch-black roads and buildings. You still need considerable depth of field, so contrary to popular opinion stop well down to at least f11. Then, with the camera on a tripod, take a series of pictures beginning with the shutter set at, say, half a second, followed by one second, and finally a whole minute. Each of these pictures will turn out to be good, but *different*.

On the first exposure the print or transparency will mainly record just the lights, with the vaguest silhouettes of buildings; the second will have more building detail, and the final one-minute frame will show not only building detail unseen by the eye, but long streaking red and white lights left by any moving vehicles that have passed by during the exposure. Headlamps will be white, taillamps red.

Bonfires, neon signs and fireworks likewise provide their own illumination, and are in fact so bright that when photographed in comparative close-up only require minimum exposure; conversely, longer exposures work just as well, probably better, by simply showing more of the same.

By and large the longer exposures are the most successful, and as it is almost impossible to overexpose because the large unlit areas remain blacked, there is ample room to experiment, bracketing exposures and comparing the results. A classic subject is the sort of firework display viewed from a distance, with roman candles and rockets shooting skywards. All you need to do is to stop well down and then leave the shutter open for as long as half an hour. Each firework will successively record on film, producing a fascinating pattern of superimposed explosions and colours.

Above and top: Phoenix, Arizona, at midnight. Such exposures are guesswork and the top picture was exposed for one minute at f11 and turned out to be overexposed, whereas the bottom picture resulted from ½ minute at f11.

Left: Las Vegas by night. Taken on un-corrected daylight-type film and on a Canon A-1 camera set on automatic exposure.

69

Process Your Own

There is nothing magical or even deeply technical about developing your own films. The prime requirement is to be able to work accurately, and to follow the film and chemical instructions with care. Colour processing is only more demanding than black-and-white in that there are more stages of development; these, like all laboratory or darkroom requirements, demand consistent temperatures and precise timing.

Three types of film need to be considered: black-and-white negative, colour negative and colour positive or reversal; each requires a different type of chemical treatment but using the same basic tools and equipment.

Only two chemicals are required for black-and-white film processing, developer and fixer, both of which are cheap and can be either home-mixed or bought in ready-mixed concentrate form. Home-mixed black-and-white chemicals will last up to three months kept in a cool dark place but deterioration does take place and concentrates which you water down as you need them, and throw away after use, tend to work out both cheaper and more consistent for the sporadic user.

Whichever type of film you use, you will need a developing tank. This is a light-tight container with an internal spiral into which the film is loaded,

The developing tank (below left) should have sufficient chemicals to cover adequately the spiral holding the film and should be agitated well to displace air bubbles from the film surface that would stop development taking place. Disposable chemicals must be poured away (below), not re-used, whereas fixer can be poured back into a container, using a funnel (bottom right), and later re-used.

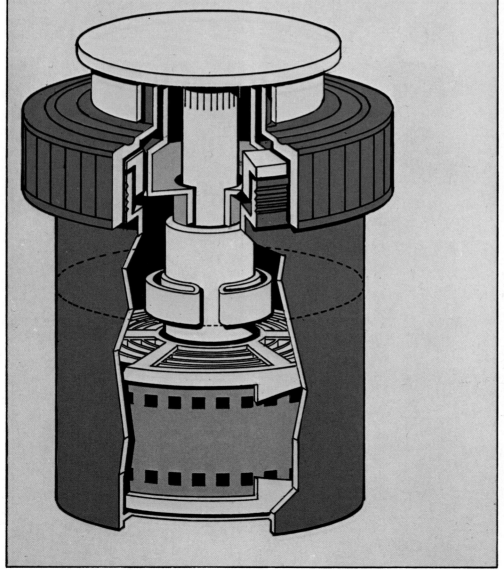

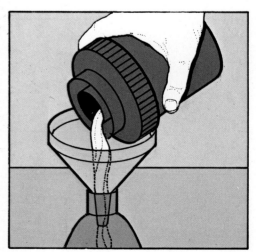

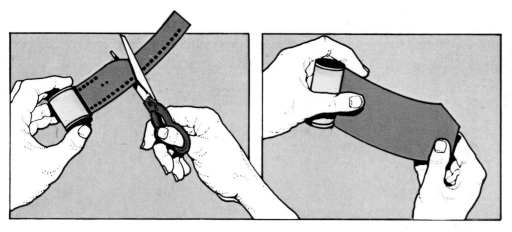

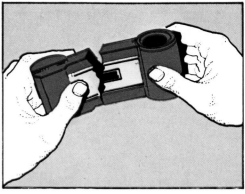

Trim the 35-mm tongue off and chamfer the sharp leading edge before attempting to load the film.

Roll films have a paper light-proof backing which is longer and covers the actual film. Separate this in the darkroom and dispose of it.

The Instamatic cartridge must be broken apart in the darkroom or changing bag for access to the actual film.

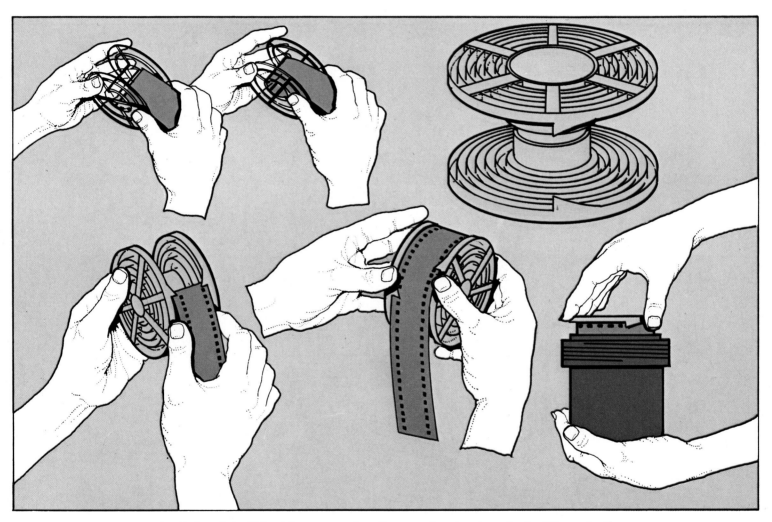

Before insertion into the processing tank the film has to be wound onto a spiral, made of nylon, plastic or stainless steel. Some spirals (top left) have to be wound from the centre outwards. Others (top right and bottom row) have to be fed from the outside and have rotating sides. In both cases care must be taken that no part of the film is in contact with another.

and a light-tight lid with an opening for pouring in chemicals. The spiral, which needs to be loaded in total darkness, holds the coiled-up film apart so that it cannot stick together once it is wet and so deny access to the chemicals. After loading the lid is fixed, and from then onwards the process can take place in daylight.

Before you actually attempt to develop your very first roll of film it is worth wasting a spare roll on a practice run, loading the spiral in daylight. Roll films come with a light-proof paper backing to protect the emulsion during loading and unloading the camera. This must be peeled off and thrown away. However, more than one innocent beginner has attempted in the dark to process this backing paper rather than the film!

Because 35-mm films are much longer, they tend to be harder to load into a spiral, so practise this with a scrap roll of film in daylight, without looking. After each practice, carefully inspect the spiral to see if the film at any point has either kinked or jumped a rail, for should either error happen during processing, the pictures at those points would stick together and be ruined.

Although you don't actually need a complete photographic darkroom for developing, you must have somewhere to load in total darkness. An adequate substitute is a changing bag, which acts rather like a tiny portable darkroom. These are cheap to buy and therefore hardly worth attempting to make, and simply consist of a light-tight bag with, at one end, a double flapped-over cover concealing a zip entrance through which we place the film or films and the whole tank assembly. At the other end of the bag are two reversed armholes like a jacket turned inside out, elasticated to make a seal and prevent lights from getting in when we place our arms in the bag to begin loading the tank.

Finally, there are the chemicals and some other small items of equipment to consider. Chemicals come complete with instructions on how to mix them, also the order they should be mixed in and at what temperature. These instructions must be strictly adhered to, for some chemicals become soluble with each other and water only above a certain temperature; below this they will neither mix nor work, so one essential aid is a thermometer.

The timing of each stage of development is critical and should be accurately taken from the moment you are pouring the chemical into the tank until the moment you empty it. A good clock-timer is a real asset, preferably one with a luminous second hand so that it can also be used later in the darkroom.

When the process and wash is over you will need a squeegee, which is like a pair of car windscreen-wipers fixed together, to wipe off the wet film. Any heavy droplets allowed to remain will leave a ring or drying mark as they recede and finally dry off. The squeegee should be kept scrupulously clean, for when wet the film emulsion is soft and easily damaged, and one grain of dirt on the squeegee could scratch the entire film length. House the squeegee in a polythene bag when you aren't using it.

Once the film has been treated, it can be hung up in a dust-free room or a clothes-drying cabinet and left to dry. You can speed drying with a portable hair-dryer, but remember that dust and fingerprints are the enemy. Use either purpose-made film clips or wooden clothes pegs for hanging up the damp film by the ends. Another way to speed drying *and* ensure that the films dry out evenly is to dip the film after washing into a weak solution of washing-up liquid and water or alternatively into one of meths and water.

HOW THE DEVELOPING PROCESS WORKS

Film emulsion is made up of silver halide grains mixed in a layer or layers of gelatine; most colour films have three such layers, each with a dye-type of colour filter built in. When silver halide grains receive light they change chemically, and the purpose of development is to blacken those areas of grain that have been attacked by light and to wash away the remainder, leaving the image. Grain areas that have received a lot of light change more than those that have received less, giving a picture its highlight or shadow areas.

The surplus silver halide grains are insoluble in water, however, and on their own would not wash away. What the developer does is change the chemical composition of those grains affected by light from silver halide to metallic silver, attacking each grain suspended in the gelatine. Those grains which have not received light remain unaffected, while the partly affected grains are attacked and reduced in size. At this stage the image is not yet stable and could still be affected by light; so it must be fixed, which is the second stage of the developing process.

The fixing agent is a chemical solvent which first kills off any developing agent left in the emulsion to stop further development, and then makes the unwanted silver halide grains soluble. The fixer does not affect the silver grains that have received light and make up the image, but the processed film now requires washing in running water to remove the newly solvent and surplus silver halide grains. The washing process is a most important stage and should not be rushed; without it the image would eventually turn brown and fade away.

Colour processing techniques follow exactly the same lines, but as there are more layers and dyes or dye couplers involved, there are more processing stages to undergo before completion. Let us look at some of the chemical problems and see how best to control them.

Gelatine, which forms the basis of all emulsions, is a relatively unstable element when wet. It swells and even liquifies and runs if it becomes too warm, or alternatively shrinks and cracks when too cold. Hence the temperature at the wet stage is critical, for any movement by the gelatine would destroy the image.

Another complication is that it takes some time for either water or chemical to soak up into gelatine, or to be replaced by the next chemical in the process, and this delay affects the time each development stage takes. We agitate the spiral during the processing to speed the soaking, move any air bubbles, and make sure that the film surface is always covered by fresh chemicals.

It is worth pre-washing the film, in other words pouring water at the correct processing temperature into the development tank to allow the emulsion to become soft and receptive before development actually starts. And after each stage of development we should use what is known as a stop

A simple way of maintaining chemical temperatures during development is to stand them in such a tray filled with a larger volume of water with provision to add hot or cold as required. Inset here is a typical small electric heating element, preferably thermostatically controlled, which acts as an immersion heater in this water-filled box.

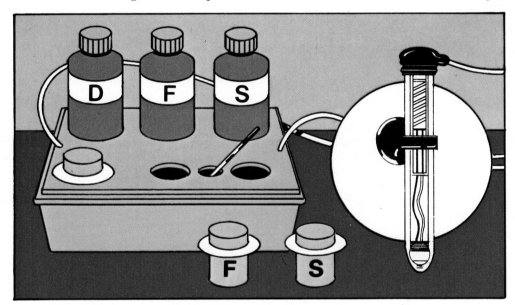

D developer
F fixer
S stop bath

bath, made up of 2% acetic acid added to the amount of water necessary to fill the developer tank. The stop bath, as the name implies, stops the development agent in its tracks, and its real purpose along with the pre-wash is to enable you to be more precise in your timing. There is an additional side benefit in that it reduces pollution in reusable chemicals.

Though neither is essential, if you process without a stop bath or pre-wash, and developer is poured straight into the tank, some of the development time is wasted whilst the film soaks up the chemical. If you remember that it can also take up to half a minute to pour the chemicals in, then on a three- or four-minute process you can no longer be accurate.

Once the first stage of development is over, it will take a further half-minute to pour out and then pour in the next chemical, which itself takes a while to displace its predecessor retained in the gelatine. During this time the total error may have grown to almost two minutes. But if you use a stop bath, which chemically works quicker and totally stops development, then it no longer matters how long it takes to pour in the next chemical, or how long that chemical takes to begin to work.

Many beginners fail even after successfully coming through the chemical stages. They then overlook the fact that gelatine is still just as unstable if there is temperature variation in the washing water, which must also be compatible. Obtaining and retaining the correct chemical and water temperatures can be a real problem for the home darkroom. Remember, heated chemicals or water will be cooling during the development process itself if their working temperature is greater than the room temperature.

The time you allow for processing depends on the temperature, and any cooling during the process should really be corrected by extending the

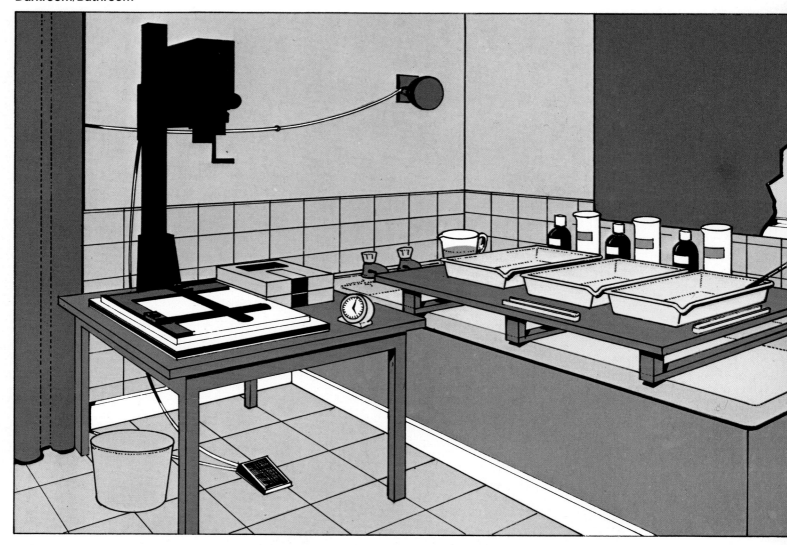

development time. Obviously this cannot be done exactly because you cannot know the precise rate of cooling or what effect it is having.

One answer for the home processor or printer is to heat a considerable volume of water, say in the kitchen sink or even in the bath, to the required processing heat and then to stand the developing tank in it; this greater volume of water will hold its temperature far longer than a small tankful.

There are many different types and makes of developer available for black-and-white films. The best by and large are the fine-grain versions; each bottle or can comes complete with a development timetable and temperature chart for all films. These charts or recommendations will refer to a gamma figure: this is the symbol used by an international scale for measuring contrast, and usually the instructions recommend processing to a contrast point of between ·5 and ·7. The higher the figure, the higher the image contrast – and, incidentally, the visible grain structure.

It is a popular misconception that when the camera operator has inadvertently, or even deliberately, underexposed, he or she can still save the picture by overdeveloping, the idea being that this in effect increases the basic film speed. Unfortunately, film density is entirely a product of its exposure to light, and overprocessing can only increase contrast and, eventually, the chemical fog level. If the negative is underexposed and some areas have not received enough light, then developing for a week won't change that. All that happens is an initial steady increase in contrast followed by chemical fogging which in due course blackens the whole image.

One reason for the misconception is that the speed rating given to any film is fairly arbitrary, intended as a guide to help produce a result, and there is a degree of latitude on either side of that figure. You can cheat a little, therefore, by using up or stretching this latitude, which sometimes can be partially disguised by processing to a higher gamma (contrast) figure. All you have really done in the process is to give the chemical longer to attack those silver halide grains which have received a minimum of light,

A simple bathroom darkroom where a bath full of warm or hot water acts as a heater to keep the chemicals up to temperature in the dishes above. These dishes, left to right, are developer, stop bath and fixer, and the finished prints can be washed in the bath water at approximately 68°F (20°C) afterwards. One word of caution: keep all electrical leads well away from water.

and at the same time allow those grains that have received a little more light to turn jet black rather than grey, hence the initial increase in contrast.

As always, there is a price to pay, for development times are calibrated, not just on the basis of how long the chemical needs to do its job, but also how long the gelatine will remain stable when wet. Given an extended development time the silver halide grains, which have a magnetic effect on each other, tend to move closer within the gelatine – a phenomenon known as clumping – and this produces a very grainy negative.

PRINTING AND ENLARGING

At this stage you do need a darkroom. This is much easier to arrange than many beginners seem to think: virtually any room will do, though preferably one with a source of running water. Don't worry if you haven't got a suitable room with running water, the wash stages can be done in daylight or elsewhere at the end of the printing operation.

Once a room is designated, you then need some form of light-proof cover for the windows and doors. Black roofing felt or a double layer of black polythene sheeting will do very well. Stretch it over a simple wooden frame and clip this in position so that it overlaps the window. Use a heavy black drape to cover any doors, and the conversion is complete. Check the effectiveness of the blackout by standing in the darkened room for at least five minutes; by then your eyes will be accustomed to the darkness and you will be able to spot any other chinks of light that you will need to deal with. Around windows, foam rubber stuck to the wooden frame can make an excellent sealer. Should you be unable to achieve total success in daylight, then wait until after dark to start work.

The developing chemicals used for printing are weaker versions of those needed for the films. Mix enough to provide a liquid depth in your dishes of about 25 mm (1 inch). You will need a minimum of three dishes, preferably four if the wash stage is to be completed elsewhere. They should be at least one size larger than the intended print, to allow room for your hands, and made of enamel or stainless steel. The latter last virtually for ever, but don't reflect as much light in the darkroom as enamel, making it a little harder to judge the exposure densities of your prints. If you think of economizing by using small dishes for small prints, remember that the chemical bulk is also small and allows rapid cooling and deterioration. The ideal compromise is to have two sets of dishes to suit all print sizes.

As with the developing stage, you need a thermometer and timing clock, also a safelight so that you can see what is going on. Paper emulsions are not all that sensitive and can be processed in quite bright yellow, orange or red light. Although the easiest way is to exchange the household overhead lamp for a low-wattage coloured bulb, it is better if the safelight is directly over the dishes. You then don't have to work in your own shadow, and you retain your normal lighting for inspecting prints. A portable safelight is therefore recommended.

To make contact prints all you need is a carrier to hold the bromide paper in close contact with the negatives, emulsion sides facing. This can be set up under the safelight. To expose, you merely turn on the normal bright room light for approximately ten seconds.

Before you begin developing, one word of warning: most people use their fingers to agitate the paper, and although printing chemicals are mild in strength they can cause or aggravate dermatitis, so if in doubt use either rubber gloves or print tongs.

After putting the paper into the developer, you rock the dish gently back and forth, exactly as you agitated the film, to disperse bubbles and to keep fresh developer on the paper surface while you watch for the image to appear. The real secret of successful printing, whether to produce contacts or enlargements, is to make the exposure just sufficient to take the developer a full two minutes to complete its process. Too much exposure, and the print's image will almost leap up out of the dish, and will be worthless. Seen under light it will lack both tone and any *total* black, which is what gives any print its true finish. If a print has been correctly exposed, its density will not alter significantly even after the two-minute development time; if it were left for up to three minutes, all that would begin to happen would be chemical fogging, as occurs when processing film.

Printing paper comes in varying grades of contrast to suit the negative.
Top left: Grade 1 is too soft for this negative.
Bottom left: Grade 2 is correct.
Top right: Grade 3 is too hard.
Bottom right: The final print on Grade 2, with the dark areas of the Houses of Parliament held back or shaded and the clock and tower burnt in.

Printing paper comes in different grades of contrast, and in many different surfaces and thicknesses; it can even be bought coated onto plastic rather than paper, which incidentally dries much quicker. Weights or thickness and surface textures are a matter of personal preference. Some people always like glossy prints while others prefer textured or matt. Whichever you choose, the developing and printing remain the same. Remember, though, to make the most of the contrast grades. These can vastly affect the end result.

If the camera exposure was perfect, and featured a subject of genuinely average contrast, which had then been accurately developed to an average-contrast or gamma ratio, such as .6, then that negative should be normal and print on normal or Grade 2 paper. However, subject contrast varies considerably from frame to frame. Consecutive pictures may be backlit, sidelit and then frontlit, in which case you will almost certainly need to make final corrections at the printing stage. A hard or contrasting negative requires a soft paper (Grade 1, or even 0) to return it to normal, while a soft subject with little contrast would need brightening up with a hard paper (Grades 3, 4, 5).

It is quite simple to judge which grade you need. You do this by inspecting the negative against a light source to check whether it has an even range of tones, with good blacks and clear areas. If there is a predominance either way, this requires correction. Grades 1, 2 and 3 should suffice to begin with, since the others are really extremes. And if you have followed the rules for exposure and development, most of your pictures should print on normal paper.

The enlarger is simply a tool to print up negatives to a size far greater than that of the actual film format, but if you are going to buy one you should proceed with care. In essence the enlarger is a reversed camera, but with a greater close-up focusing range, and an electric light bulb or cold cathode ray tube to provide a light source for projection. The negative is placed in exactly the same position as it occupies in the camera, and its image is projected by the light source down on to a base board which holds the printing paper. The size of enlargement is controlled by raising or lowering the enlarger unit to increase or decrease the size of the projected image.

Good optics, as with a camera, are essential. Fortunately, enlarger lenses are both cheaper and easier to change than those used in cameras. Format size is also important. You can have either a universal enlarger, which will accept virtually any negative size, or an instrument designed and built specifically for one format.

Enlarger lenses need to be compatible with the negative size, with a diagonal measurement close to that of the negative. For instance, a 75-mm lens will be correct for 6 x 6 cm roll film and a 50-mm lens for a 35-mm film. This lens length matters because, like the camera, although the process is in reverse, longer or shorter lenses would require an inconvenient and maybe even impossible amount of up-and-down movement on the enlarger.

Condenser diffuser enlarger

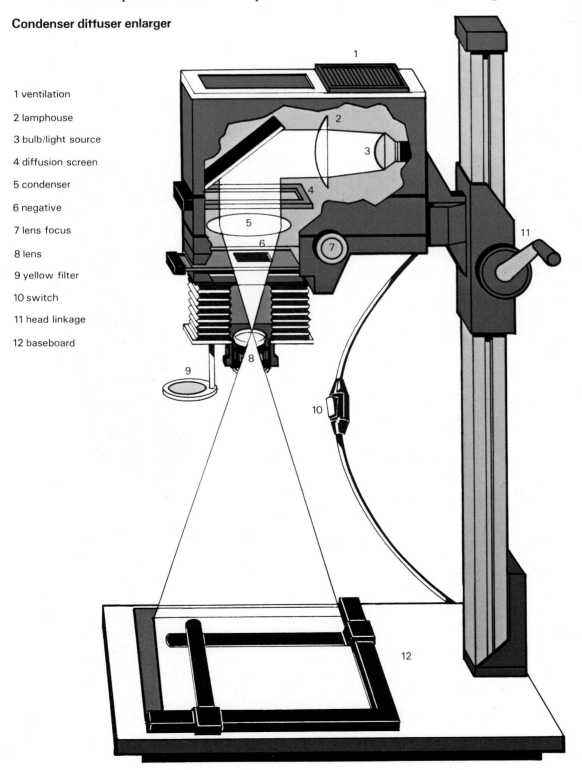

1 ventilation

2 lamphouse

3 bulb/light source

4 diffusion screen

5 condenser

6 negative

7 lens focus

8 lens

9 yellow filter

10 switch

11 head linkage

12 baseboard

A good example of a tungsten-lit enlarger. The light source is well away from the film or negative so that its heat will neither buckle nor damage.

To project their illumination evenly, bulb enlargers use additional condenser lenses which both arrange the light source and also protect the negative from damaging heat. These are placed between the light source and the negative, and they too must relate to the lens and format size. This means that universal enlargers must have a set of condensers as well as an enlarger lens for each size of negative used. Even then, the bulb type of universal enlarger is at best a jack-of-all-trades and master of none.

Cold cathode enlargers pass light evenly and run at a cooler temperature and so do not need the extra condensers. But if the normal film size is constant, an enlarger designed specifically for that size alone tends to be far more precise.

To produce a print, the negative image is projected onto the enlarger base board and the lens panel moved until the image is in sharp focus. This focusing operation can be considerably helped by a focusing aid, available for a few pence from photo shops, which is rather like a magnified periscope. The aid is placed on the base board, and via an eyepiece magnifies a tiny part of the image to enormous proportions, so that you can actually focus on the grain structure of the film.

Focusing is done with the lens set wide open, to give the brightest image for ease of viewing. However, all lenses have some depth of field and this can lead to human error at the focusing stage, so after focusing stop down approximately two stops to the working aperture.

Next, you either switch off the enlarger or, better still, blank off the light source with a red filter, which is usually provided beneath the lens, and place the paper onto the masking frame or holder. Now you are ready to make the first print. Switch on or uncover the lens so that light is now projecting directly onto the paper emulsion (the shiny face of the printing paper), and allow about 20 seconds for a test exposure.

Holding back or shading and burning in can be done by using one's hands on larger areas, but it is important that the printer keeps his hands moving so as to avoid casting a definite shadow image.

Exposure times are arbitrary with enlargers, and best learned by experience. (There are now enlarger exposure meters similar to those used with cameras, but they are fairly expensive and still require some human judgment.) Every combination of negative and paper grade will need a different exposure time, which you will soon learn to gauge. To begin with, try cutting up a sheet of paper into strips and use these for exposure tests rather than waste a whole sheet each time.

The real secret of successful printing, whether it be contacts or enlargements, is that the exposure should be just sufficient to take the developer a *full* two minutes to complete its process.

After two minutes of agitation in the developing dish the now-wet print or strip should be transferred, left to right, to a stop bath containing water mixed with 2% acetic acid; from there it goes to the final fixer dish. Provided a stop bath has been used, then normal top lighting can be switched on the moment the print is in the fixer. Without a stop bath, the print should be given a minute or two for the fixer to act before the top lighting is switched on. Precaution: make sure your boxes of printing paper have been closed!

It is important to view in good light – as opposed to even the brightest safelight – for prints that often look good to the inexperienced in dim light can be seen to be miles out as soon as they are viewed under full illumination.

Much of the photographer's craft can be learned and carried further in the darkroom. You can alter the cropping of a negative, and even overprint certain areas or hold back others, even double print, and dramatically change the visual impact.

A simple example is the old Victorian vignetting effect where the print corners are lightened by projecting the image through a hole cut in a second sheet of printing paper, which cuts off the light which would otherwise reach the corners. For the best results, hold the paper in space somewhere between the enlarger head and the base board, and keep it gently moving. This avoids a clearly defined edge being projected and produces the characteristic fading effect.

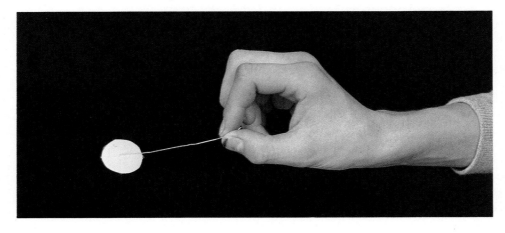

Better than hands for holding light back from part of a print are such simply made dodgers.

Similarly, you can overprint any area, either by cupping your hands to the desired shape or by using a pre-cut sheet as before to light that area where you want more exposure. This is easier to achieve on a long exposure time, so stop the lens right down to extend the duration and give yourself more time to work.

First expose the whole negative, then on a second exposure of probably equal duration, print in those specific areas that need more. Using the holed paper, you can burn in images of any size, from tiny objects such as a face in a group to large areas such as an entire sky.

Conversely, there are many times when one object or part of a picture goes too dark, even on a single short exposure. Here you can save the situation by what is known as dodging, or holding light back from one part of the print. To make your own dodgers, take a few lengths of fairly fine piano wire approximately 30 cm (12 inches) long and bend one end into a small ring. Next, cut out a series of potentially useful shapes from black card, or even pre-fogged printing paper (which will not reflect), and tape the cut-offs to the ringed ends of the wires. Dodging should be done in one long exposure. Remember to keep the dodger moving, including the wire which might otherwise record on the print in shadow form.

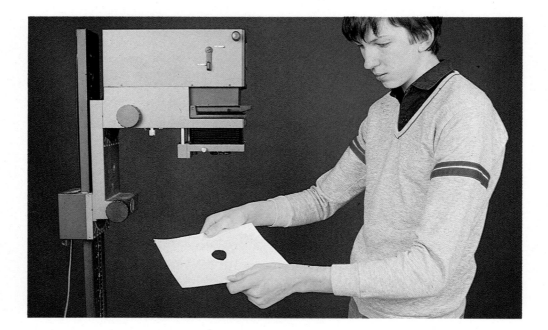

To burn in small areas cut a hole in card to the shape required and then give those under-exposed areas an extra exposure.

WASHING AND DRYING

Washing and drying prints in volume can pose considerable problems for the home darkroom. The simple answer is to leave the prints after fixing in a water-filled dish (the fourth dish) for attention later. When the rest of your tasks are done, you can wash the prints properly in a bath or sink; make sure you move them around occasionally so that they do not stick together.

Another, better way is to buy a proprietary print washer. These work much like a film spiral, but are designed in drawer form to keep the prints apart. All you then need is running water, supplied by hosepipe from the nearest tap, and some means of drainage which you can provide by standing the whole assembly in a bath or sink. Print washing can then continue unaided and unwatched for the required twenty minutes.

Successful drying is more difficult. Any uneven drying marks will show, as with film, so first squeegee the surplus water off the print surface until no droplets are present. If no other method is available the prints can then be quite literally hung up with clothes pegs to dry. The snags with this method, apart from unfavourable weather, are that as the paper dries it tends to curl up, and gloss paper dried naturally finishes up as semi-gloss.

Conventional bromide paper that has been thoroughly soaked, really needs a proprietary drier or glazer to dry it out evenly and give it a pro-fessional finish. Driers consist of a large metal box with a curved top; inside are electric-fire heating elements, and a canvas cover can be pulled tight over the top.

With matt or semi-gloss prints, you place them face up on the curved top-plate, and then pull the canvas hard down to hold the prints flat and soak up any remaining surface water; leave the heat from the elements to do the rest. For a high-gloss or glazed surface, insert a chromium-plated sheet face up on top of the drier and place the prints face (or emulsion) down on top of the chrome sheet. Roller the prints firmly with a rubber roller and then pull the canvas over.

The roller is important, for as the prints are face down any surface water will turn to steam which will lift the print face off the chrome plate, leaving an unglazed bubble. When the prints are totally dry and therefore glazed, you will hear them cracking off the chromium plate; do not be tempted to peel them off any earlier, because the emulsion is sticking to the hot sheet and would tear.

A simpler alternative is to use plastic printing paper which cannot absorb water; only the emulsion, which holds little liquid, needs to be dried, and the overall drying time is greatly reduced. Although this type of print could be left face up to dry off unaided, there are simple machines through which the finished but still-wet print can be fed over heated rollers or past a hot-air blower, reappearing fully dry on the other side after only seconds. The drawbacks to this method are the expense of the paper and a lack of surface or contrast choices. However, it is the 'paper' of the future and much easier to work with.